Lyman Beecher Lectures on Preaching
Yale University, 1917

GOOD MINISTERS OF JESUS CHRIST

By
WILLIAM FRASER McDOWELL

One of the Bishops
of the
Methodist Episcopal Church

THE ABINGDON PRESS

NEW YORK   CINCINNATI

CONTENTS

PERSONAL FOREWORD

FOR more than a generation I have been reading the Yale Lectures as the successive volumes have appeared, reading them with an ever-growing profit and interest. On my way to be a student in the School of Theology I carried with me to read on the train the lectures of both Brooks and Simpson, then recently published. Through the years since then these and other volumes have helped to keep my ideals fresh, my standards from sagging, and my vision of the ministry clear and attractive before my own eyes. For twenty-five years I have been out of the pastorate, in positions which by their very nature tend to make a person official and administrative in his attitude and spirit. These lines, perhaps all too personal for such a place, are intended to suggest what they cannot express, an undying and increasing gratitude to the men and the influences that have helped to preserve for me, in my ministry through the years, "the vision splendid."

The gracious invitation to serve as Lyman Beecher lecturer in this year brought more than ordinary embarrassment just because of this

long and devoted use of the lectures given by
other men. What they have said so well, what
has soaked into me, what has been absorbed by
me must surely reappear in every one of these
chapters. I am entirely willing to have it so,
but other men must not be held responsible,
even though their influence can be seen and
felt in every page, an influence that is large
and real, but cannot be indicated in detail. It
would be easy to make pedantic display in the
way of references, but this would be no more
attractive here than it is in sermons. So this
broad and grateful acknowledgment is set
down here at the beginning, the acknowledgment of a lifelong indebtedness to multitudes
of "men and books."

These addresses were prepared and delivered
in a time of unparalleled "storm and stress" in
the world, a time in which everything is thought
of as affected by the unspeakable war. Men
naturally wonder what kind of world we shall
live in, what kind of ministry will serve the
world and how it will serve it, and even what
sort of Christianity will exist when the war is
over. The very life of Christ's kingdom seems
involved in this world crash. Men can scarcely
think or speak of anything else. "All our talking and thinking have become like the open
page of a monthly magazine, with a bloody

smear, a thing of red and black dragged across it." Nevertheless, the war is not at all prominent in these lectures. It has been my eager desire to see and my earnest endeavor to present a ministry that might be worthy and vital while war lasts and when war has passed, as it will pass; to lay hold for our ministry of principles steadfast and eternal even in the day when the earth is rocking under our feet. I dare not think that I have succeeded as the subject deserves, but in putting the ministry of the Master in its spirit, purpose, and essence under the ministry of men in these troubled days I dare believe that I have tried to do what is well for us all.

The wish to do this explains all that is said and all that is omitted. His ministry is constantly treated in these studies as both an event that occurred and a principle that ever abides. His life in its deepest meanings is held to contain the essential principles of all human life. He himself is regarded both as pattern and power for men. I desire the ministry of the Master to lie in power under, around, above, and within the ministry of the men of our own and later days.

For the dear church of which I am a minister, for my "brethren and companions" and for myself I make hearty but inadequate expression of appreciation of the invitation given by Yale University to attempt this service and for the generous hospitalities and gracious courtesies extended to me during the delivery of these addresses. Substantially as they were spoken the lectures are now offered to the larger world in the humble hope that they may add at least some small amount to that large and distinguished service rendered to the church and the world through more than two centuries by "Yale, the mother of men," and help to make the ministry of men in real measure one in spirit and purpose with the ministry of the everliving Master of men.

Washington, District of Columbia,
April twenty-sixth,
One thousand nine hundred and seventeen.

LECTURE I
THE MINISTRY OF REVELATION
"Show us the Father."

LECTURE I

THE MINISTRY OF REVELATION

WE have come up to study and possibly to
write another chapter on the work of preaching
and the life of the preacher; to consider again
our ministry to the world we live in; to take
counsel together as to our lives, our message,
and our methods; to take another look at our
task and our resources; to refresh ourselves in
fellowship with one another and with our Elder
Brother; to compare our hopes with our experiences, our achievements with our ideals; to
mingle as in one family, younger brothers looking eagerly forward, meeting with older brothers
whose work is partly done. It is not an experience wholly full of comfort to those who are
no longer young. Coming to deliver a half
dozen addresses on preaching seems to one who
assumes to do it somewhat like coming to a
day of judgment, where one meets the deeds
already done, the noble plans abandoned, neglected, or imperfectly fulfilled; the high ideals
unrealized in practice; where the man that is
faces the man that meant to be and wishes he
could have a second probation. I suspect that

13

we older men are looking for our second probation in you younger ones, hoping to find in you a success that we have missed in ourselves. We have a hope that something may be made of you, being caught young. And we have a sincere desire to help you get at the beginning the direction, the tone your ministry should keep until its end.

Strangely enough, I do not find myself troubled by coming into this noble succession so late. It staggers and humbles me to come into it at all, but it must have been an appalling task to plan the first course of lectures on this foundation. Everything had to be said! But now, as after-dinner orators say, so much has been said, and so well said, that it can be taken for granted. It is not necessary to put into one brief series all that could be said upon the general subject or upon any portion of it. We may have the same comforting assurance in our preaching. A preacher need not feel obliged to say in one sermon all that could be said upon chosen text or topic. We may safely and wisely assume what has been said before us and what will be said after us. There have been and there will be other sermons. This reflection has large incidental advantages to a congregation. So there have been other lectures, and doubtless there will be other lectures, as the years pass.

"Wherefore let us comfort one another with these words."

This consideration, with others, permits a proper limitation of our theme. The enlarged scope of the modern ministry tends somewhat to confusion. When this Lyman Beecher lectureship was founded the minister was distinctly preacher and pastor to a single congregation. That was the dominant type. Upon that type everything was built. We have seen an immense extension of the idea of the ministry, until we can no longer assume that all students in a seminary are looking forward to the form of ministry which was once supreme and almost exclusive. The dreams of men are based upon the experiences of men. And it comes to pass that many young ministers are looking forward to becoming teachers of theology or other subjects, social workers, reformers, professional evangelists, editors, secretaries of benevolent boards, administrators of religious affairs and activities—all of them forms of life in which the ministry of service is real, but in which preaching may be and often is slight and occasional, and pastoral functions entirely lacking. It is very interesting to note the number of men sustaining the ministerial relation, and presumably fulfilling the ministerial function, who are satisfying their call to the ministry in

these special ways. And it is also interesting
to note the provision we have made for the
training of men and the service of men with
this enlarged conception of the ministry in
view. Compare, for example, the curriculum
of this institution when Henry Ward Beecher
first spoke on this foundation with the curriculum of this year. Compare the Plymouth
Church of 1867 with the St. George's or Plymouth Church of 1917, and you will see the
distance we have come. Our provisions for
perfecting the saints have become very abundant.

Now, with all this extension we may well
have the fullest sympathy, but in these few
hours together our concern is emphatically with
the minister who is preacher to a congregation
and pastor to a community. Other subjects
are interesting, other activities useful, but only
in a secondary and related sense do they come
within the scope of our studies together. In
other words, we do not propose to consider
everything ministers may do and still fulfill
their ministry, though that might be interesting and valuable. There will be a lot of true
things to say after we are through. It is
enough for us to speak the truth on this more
limited basis.

I choose this special field with the firm conviction that there is no relation in the world which is nobler, happier, or more useful than this specific relation. Knowing full well all the charms and attractions, all the possibilities and opportunities that lie in other relations and forms of service; being personally familiar with more than one of these special forms of activity, and being deeply concerned for your highest happiness and highest usefulness, I cannot ask of God anything better for you through long years than such a relation, such a ministry, in town or country, in city or village. I know the current talk upon the subject, but after all is said the world has nothing finer in opportunity or reward to offer to any man than this kind of ministry, in the Master's name, to a given community.

Principal Selbie said lately to a gathering of theological students that what would matter in their future lives was the work they did in their own churches, that the work they did outside their churches would amount to very little.

This will bring you to the concrete question, what kind of minister you really intend and plan to be. Preaching and being a preacher may be vague and indefinite or clear and definite. The real greatness of the conception must not be lost either in vagueness or in narrowness. We must save our souls from littleness by breadth, and from haziness by definiteness like our Master's.

I have chosen the particular theme, "Good Ministers of Jesus Christ," in order to base the whole theory and practice of our ministry upon the ministry of Jesus Christ. The fundamental basis upon which I rest all these studies is this: His ministry was both a fact and a perpetual example, both an event in time and a principle to live by for all time, a thing of glory in itself and a thing of supreme worth forevermore. It was once and is always. It could not be the event it was without also being a principle. Nor could we get the principles we require except in a fact like his life and ministry. Our ideals must root in reality. The good minister of Jesus Christ ought as far as possible be a minister like Jesus Christ. Make all proper allowances for his unique purpose and work, his unique character and life, for his sinlessness and his Lordship, for the manifest differences between his ministry and ours, between his life and ours, still the discovery of possible resemblances in spirit, principle, and purpose is more important than finding the differences. What he tried to do the modern minister must substantially try to do. What he essentially was the modern minister must essentially be. For the keynote of our ministry

18

we must use his own most significant words:
"The kingdom of heaven is like." Not that we
are like him in sufficient measure, but this is
what we ought to be. We do not truly exalt
him to his true and supreme place by giving
him a solitary and unrelated place, no matter
how high. We wrong ourselves and our ministry by any detachment from him. We honor
him, not by drawing away, but by drawing
near, not by our differences from him, but by
our likeness to him. The ministry is to be interpreted in the light of this supreme Person
and his ministry. It is not a profession with
which we deal, but a personal life having its
roots, its inspirations and its examples, its purposes, in another personal life. These roots go
far past Liddon, Beecher, Simpson, Storrs, and
Spurgeon; far deeper than the particular ecclesiasticism in which we have our home; beyond
Oxford, or Geneva, or Boston. As men and
ministers we repeat Whittier's words:

> "O, Lord and Master of us all,
>   Whate'er our name or sign,
> We own thy sway, we hear thy call,
>   We test our lives by thine."

And we base our lives and our ministry upon
his. What we shall build the future only can
tell, but "other foundation can no man lay,
than that is laid, which is Jesus Christ." We

have thought of him as the founder, but not so much as the foundation of our ministry. Happily, you can build. You are yet young. Your ministry is not closing, but opening. Let us take heed how we build.

Men are wondering, as they have in other periods, whether Christianity is a living or a spent force in the world. The faith of many is in eclipse. Many walk in despair and darkness. They feel that one world is dead, they are not sure that a better has any power to be born. Into such an era you come. Only a ministry like his can have any message to this mad, modern world. If you come to your preaching and pastoral service as he did, clothed with the power of an endless life, then once more the heavens will open and men will see the angels of God ascending and descending.

I do not dare hope that I can accomplish what lies in my heart and desire. But I must try to make clear to you the kind of minister I am hoping to be and to see before the end of the day comes. This personal basis of the ministry, this relation of it to the ministry of Jesus, and this consciousness of him as example and fellow, keep fresh a ministry which otherwise and by its very nature tends to become administrative and official. I may not achieve the portrayal of this ministry or accomplish the radiant thing itself, but some time, somewhere somebody will. In the light of the ministry of the Master we shall some time see what the ministry of the men may be. And by his grace there may be some standing here who shall not taste of death until they see him coming again in new men like unto him.

And now what is the primary, outstanding feature of that perfect ministry upon which our own is to be based? What was the supreme demand made upon him, the supreme test applied to him, the deepest question asked him? What above everything else did he try to do? We shall find the answer to our own questions in his experience, the light for our lives in his life. For answer, open human history, religious history, preaching history, at a particular page upon which are recorded at once the supreme question and its perfect answer. A group of men is gathered about a ministering man who is saying many things to them, many wise, important, and necessary things. Never before or since was any man saying more important things. It was unequaled speech, it remains unequaled. Into the flow of this speech one of those men broke with an insistent request. He probably did not think of the universal reach of his demand; he certainly did not know that it would get into print and cut through the centuries, speaking for men, speaking to men in all times and lands. But this word of Philip to Jesus walks at large in the history of humanity and religion. There is no other word that goes deeper. "Show us the Father and it sufficeth us." That was the ancient form of it, spoken for a group of earnest men. "Show us your God," said a group of modern Japanese students to a modern missionary. A heathen child said to the missionary, "What is God like?" A student preparing for the ministry wrote me two years ago: "I desire to ask if you can help me in a vital point. For some reason I cannot be assured that there is a living, personal God. I think there must be, but assurance is not mine. Can you help me? Are you *sure* that there is a God; and if so, can you tell me how I may be sure?" If, now, a ministering man in that early group or to any late group or person cannot do this thing they ask, it does not matter much what else he can do. He may speak ever so wisely upon many other vital themes, may answer many other searching and interesting questions, but if he cannot do this supreme thing, his ministry fails at its center. He must reveal God, must make God manifest and real, to common, ordinary men when life is ordinary and when it is critical. This is the test for him and for us. Philip said, "Show us

THE MINISTRY OF REVELATION

the Father." Centuries afterward, Lord Tennyson said, "I covet above all things else a fresh vision of God." "What can you tell me about God quick?" said one soldier to another in the trenches in France in the great war. He to Philip and we to Tennyson and the soldier and the student must be able to answer for life's sake, for in any age or any country this is humanity's deepest need and keenest cry. There are other questions, real and urgent, which must be answered. "If a man die, shall he live again?" "What must we do to be saved?" "What is the first, great commandment?" "Who is my neighbor?"—these and many others will crowd upon your ministry for answer. But no answer can be given to them unless that deeper question about God can first be answered. They all center in it. Woe betide the ministry that wears itself out upon the petty or the secondary questions of life, and woe betide the world when the ministry is dumb or helpless in the presence of humanity's deepest needs, or when its ministry does not know its real center or cannot make a real revelation. You remember how Wells puts it, in the words of Mr. Britling: "Religion is the first thing and the last thing, and until a man has found God and been found by God, he begins at no beginning, he works to no end.

23

He may have his friendships, his partial loyalties, his scraps of honor. But all these things fall into place, and life falls into place, only with God—God, who fights through men against Blind Force and Night and Non-Existence; who is the end, who is the meaning. He is the only King. . . . Of course I must write about him. I must tell all my world of him." Few moments in history are more critical than the moment in which Philip asks Jesus the supreme question. A form of words, however careful and sound, will not do in reply. Men are never saved by a phrase, however accurate, nor by a verbal definition, however exact. "There must always be a person open to God and knowing God, open to men and knowing men, to interpret between the two. Through a person, through Jesus perfectly, God makes his way to men." Phrase-makers have a standing which they do not deserve. It is fortunate for us all that poor Philip, perplexed and anxious, did not fall into the hands of one of them. If he had, this might have been the result: "Is it possible, Philip, that you do not know yet what I have been so careful to say over and over? Let me tell it again, then, as simply and concisely as possible. And never forget it. Pass on this statement, for it is exact: 'The Father is the Person, spiritual, good, holy, wise, powerful and loving, who creates, orders, and sustains all.'" This is adapted from Clarke's Outline of Christian Theology, and is about as good as any, but it would have left Philip pretty helpless. And it would not have gone far into human life and experience. I said so once in Dr. Clarke's own presence, not knowing that he was present. He promptly and graciously assured me that he wholly agreed with me. Then he added: "Theologians must not be required to do more than this. They can only furnish the raw materials for preachers who must make verbal things living things." Preachers must do much more than theologians. For this sort of definition can only be made in terms of life, this sort of revelation only through personality. The ministry of Jesus and the ministry of others must each make manifest and make real the personal God. Each must bring us, not a doctrine of God, but God himself. Each must be a revealing ministry, must give men, not an intellectual conception of God, but a personal perception of him. Each must be the kind of ministry that can make quick, clear, certain disclosure to Philip, to soldier in the trenches, to poet laureate, to dying man, to inquiring child, to student, or to foreigner saying, "Show us your God." This is the despair of our ministry; it is also the glory of it. For what Jesus perfectly did in his ministry he has made possible in ours. He was not helpless, he has not left us helpless. He did not fail; we must not fail to make God clear to men. This was the center of his ministry, it is the center of ours. It is easier to elaborate the doctrine of the divine nature or to marshal the proofs of the divine existence. And these tasks must ever be performed by able men. But the real problem for religion and life in the hands of the preacher is the problem of making God manifest as he is. Jesus's contribution to the world was not a proof of God's existence nor an analysis of his attributes, but a living disclosure of his face and heart. His ministry was a revealing ministry, as ours must be. It is easier to discuss God as a problem, but far more useful to reveal him as a Person, to give him to men as a living reality, to make him known to actual life. We can explain him or we can look into his face and cause other men to do it.

And our age is in sore need of a new vital vision or sense of God. It does not matter much how that statement is made. The need is always fundamental, but in our own age it is particularly acute. God is "in eclipse." God has no practical significance for a large part of the modern world. The prosperous classes think him unnecessary, the unprosperous think him useless. Scholars have eliminated him from their thinking, the ignorant from their living. He has faded out of men's lives. We are, in general, in the condition of Rugby boys of Arnold's time: "God was not in all their thoughts." We use large vague terms, like immanence and transcendence; or impersonal ones like "streams of tendency, not ourselves, making for righteousness"; or we ignore him altogether. One of the tendencies of the time, in preaching and elsewhere, has been characterized as "the marked withdrawal of emphasis from the Deity." Even the ministry has become rather ostentatiously the servant of the people and regards itself much less than formerly as the servant of God. The average man is not a philosophical atheist or agnostic. He does not use the exact terms of philosophy to define or describe his attitude. He either shrugs his shoulders or blusters wildly as he says, "I do not know." God simply does not count. A keen student puts it thus: "Faith has been hard hit in our own generation by vague, indeterminate, abstract ways of speaking of God. Matthew Arnold's 'stream of tendency' is not easily grasped by ordinary folk; still less easily worshiped. 'The First Cause,' 'The Life Force' are poor, attenuated substitutes for the God to whom our grandfathers prayed." For all practical purposes of real life these abstractions are entirely useless. They leave the average person hanging in mid-air. Where they leave the cultivated person it would be hard to say. Such terms as "immanence" and "transcendence," true as they are, have mighty little preaching value as such. And it is of the preacher that we are thinking; the minister to humanity as it is, to all kinds of humanity; the preacher who is the only man to cure present conditions, who is the only man to restore what we may call the intensity of humanity's sense of God. The preacher must do this and then guide the keen sense of personal relations into right ways. But often the preacher himself is not keenly conscious of God, either as calling him into the ministry or as giving power and authority to his ministry. The current sense of God is weak, vague, and largely mistaken. The half gods have come and are on the throne. We have new idolatries and polytheisms, conventional and official beliefs in God, vast unconsciousness of and vast indifference to him. And it does not disturb us as much as we might suppose. A thoughtful English preacher declares that this whole modern tragedy has come, first and last, because of the neglect or denial of the Christian view of God and the world. "We were too secure to feel our need of God." "Europe is without any decisive and implacable sense of the nature of God." When the sense of God is weak the obligation to be careful of his world and his children is not likely to be strong and effectual.

M. Guyau some years ago pictured a world from which God had disappeared and in which men lived contentedly without him. "We have morbid sensitiveness to pain, acute consciousness of poverty, some sense of wrong, but a dull sense of God." We are much surer that he is good and kind than our fathers were, but we are not half so sure that he is and that he is omnipotent. It takes both truths to make a whole truth. Their value depends on their being held together. This is the deepest "hurt of the daughter of my people," that modern Israel does not know as ancient Israel did. The old literature is shot through with the sense of God's immediate presence. God was supreme in the Book because he was so supreme in life. As Professor Seth put it, "God was an experience, not simply an object." Of course we know how crude and childlike much of that early thinking was. We are fond of pointing out its crudities. It belongs to an early stage of religious development to say, "The word of the Lord came," "And God said," and "The Lord appeared." We prefer to speak less plainly. But in getting rid of crudities men often get rid of realities. In refining speech to fit our nicer philosophies and more careful theologies we sometimes destroy all its personal revealing value. The mighty evangelists had no vague sense of God. They created no vague sense. Jesus himself had a keen, acute sense of God. His attitude is our model. It was not crude, though it was altogether clear and definite. It is for us to pattern both faith and practice upon the highest illustration and example. He gives us that. Why should we make so much of Jesus's consciousness of God as a proof of his deity as though that exhausted it? His rich experience was far more than an argument. It suggests and reveals possibilities in other lives. Surely, this thing that meant everything to him cannot have been exhausted in him.

The good minister of Jesus Christ must be like his Master in this matter. In certain atmospheres and conditions it is easy both to believe and to understand the fact of God's direct influence upon human life. It seems to have been easier when the world was younger and the race nearer its childhood. It is not at all hard to understand as we see it in the brief years of Jesus's ministry. We can easily believe that God was with him, that to him the word of the Lord came, but that God is with us, that the word of the Lord comes, is another matter. We can see the process going on as he moved among men. He worked it out. He did not give everybody health or wealth, but he did give them what was far better, what was altogether best. And if one really wants to know how far the life and ministry of Jesus are imitable, let him try it. Modern Christendom, the modern ministry, is nowhere near the border of fanaticism yet in its imitation of the Master in this or any other respect.

And the ministry cannot do the work of Jesus for humanity by any other way than his way. And unless it does do his work, then the world is well lost. The world is likely to be rich enough and smart enough, but a world with a vague, or dull or mistaken sense of God cannot be a right world. Men make vague prayers to a vague God, and God quickly fades when praying becomes colorless and impersonal. Men have a complacent view of sin and a futile notion of forgiveness when the sense of God is dim. The sense of personal worth and personal relations gets weak under the reign of the half gods. The consciousness of immortality becomes thin and doubtful when the sense of the Eternal God grows feeble. The power of an endless life ceases when the sense of its source decays. Efforts for human welfare are easily exhausted unless the strength of the everlasting arms is beneath them. Preaching goes wrong when there is a sapping at the springs. It loses its tone when it fails to see him face to face, when it is afraid to go into his presence. Woe to those prophets whom the Lord hath not sent, and woe to the world when being otherwise sent they pretend to speak as prophets. The men who speak by authority of everybody or anybody but God, or with authority about everything except God, speak with false or with secondary authority.

It would be difficult to name any one outstanding feature of the Bible. That book is so opulent for the purposes of personal religion and for preaching that no one word will adequately characterize it. But surely it makes the clear impression upon anyone who reads it, even in the most casual way, that it is the record of God's persistent and affectionate effort to reveal himself to human life, to get himself helpfully into human life, to become a real power in human life and to enable human beings to know him. The Gaelic language is said to have fifty words for "darling," and occasionally one person will apply them all to another person. The Bible fairly overflows, not with names for God, not with gods, but with those living terms that have permanent religious value and lasting preaching value. Of course it is such a book as it is, because it records such an effort on his part. Man's endeavor to find God, to understand him, to get on good terms with him does not begin to equal God's effort to find man, to reveal himself to man, to get into good relations with man. A ministry, therefore, that sets out to be a revealing ministry, to make God manifest and real to modern life, puts itself in line with God's own unchanging effort and purpose.

Jesus Christ was the supreme endeavor of God to make himself known. His ministry was centered around and based upon this purpose. He tried it all the time, with all sorts of people, promising and unpromising, people of keen vision and people of dull vision. He carried about with him, he created among men what has been called "an awareness of the presence of God in the world, in every part of the world and in the life of man." Of course we know the difference between him and ourselves, between his ministry and ours. We never forget that. But we too easily forget the resemblances and identities. These I am trying to emphasize. The imitation of Christ has special meaning here. And I wish we might see one luminous generation of preachers showing how far the ministry of Jesus is imitable in its essential features. We need not be afraid either of mysticism or of supernaturalism. And we need not exaggerate the benefits of Jesus's personal, earthly presence nor overestimate the achievements of his disciples while he was visibly with them. Manifestly he expected us to do better than they did both in the apprehension of truth and in the application of truth. God seemed tolerably immediate when Jesus was here. Was Jesus wrong in the expectation that God should not seem less immediate and near, but more real after he was gone? Modern Christianity, the modern ministry, has imagined itself to be deprived of some advantages that belonged to the days of the incarnation. The cry, "Back to Christ," has only been partly wise. We more than half believe that we are at disadvantage at a vital point. And the deadliest skepticism of the modern ministry is that skepticism which, not being quite sure of God, does not expect any very mighty thing to happen. We are as bad as the Nazarenes in the synagogue. And when a man sometimes with crude theology, limited culture, and raw methods, but with keen sense of God's immediate presence, does some overwhelming thing in spite of his limitations, we go to discussing him and ask again, "Is not this Joseph's son?" And it

all does happen when a man takes a dead letter
up into living hands, changes the emphasis to
the personal terms and declares: "The Spirit of
the Lord is upon me, because he hath anointed
me." The cure for ordinariness is not sensa-
tionalism, but true supernaturalism. There are
men who appear to think that a big rich church
makes God practically unnecessary, and that
God himself cannot do anything worth while in
a small, poor one. In one case material complacency is the result, in the other case utter
depression. God is not considered seriously in
either case. God is not in the problem as a
factor, or if in it at all, only as un unknown
quantity or as a conventional element.

Many men have felt and pointed out how a
thousand things tend to blur the sense of God
in a preacher's life: such as drudgery, pain,
sorrow, poverty, prosperity, age, illness, victory
in battle for reform, defeat in battle for reform,
and the desire to avoid dogmatism. Keeping
the sense of God keen and fresh, retaining the
power to see "the vision splendid," enriching
the enthusiasm of youth by the riper experience
of the middle watch and still keeping the purple
glow upon it, preserving the thrill after twenty-
five years' hard pounding on the nerves—all
this is difficult beyond words. You may fail
to do it and may still have a respectable and

useful, but a wholly conventional and un-prophetic, ministry. There will be no burning bushes, no opening heavens, no live coals touching speaking lips, no voice saying, "This is my Son."

In Conclusion

. Now, how can a man's ministry become a revealing ministry in any real sense? What impression did Jesus make about God? How did he do it? What impression can a modern minister make, in line with the ministry of Jesus? How can he do it? This is not asking what statements can be made about God, nor what creed can be elaborated concerning him. It is asking, with the country church, the metropolitan church, the college, the shop, the mine, the kindergarten, the heathen world in view, how the minister of to-day can make God real to all this human life. The creation of eternal life is the end, knowledge of God the only means. How can it be done? If we are to get Jesus's results, we must surely follow Jesus's way. Other foundation for our ministry can no man lay. Any other foundation will give way. A good many men are wondering whether Christianity has run its course, whether it has become outworn, whether it is still to be a force in the world, whether the ministry has any living word to say. I can see but one answer to all these questions and fears. The ministry of Jesus was a revealing ministry because he knew God, because he was like God in character and purpose, and because he faithfully presented this God whom he knew, whom he was like, to the people about him—to the dull people, the narrow people, the argumentative people, and all the rest. And if our ministry is to be a revealing ministry, it must be by these same methods. The minister must know him, the minister must be like him, the minister must show him as he is. Do not exaggerate, do not put false or extravagant meaning into these words. I know the dangers that lie in every such statement, but I know also the far deadlier danger that lies in a ministry that does not know him, is not like him in character, and does not reveal him in any true and living way. Practical agnosticism is the worst sort in the world except pulpit agnosticism. A ministry afraid of the supreme venture is a poor, futile thing in the world's life.

Now, I think by the aid of three questions it will be possible to set this out clearly:

Whom do you know best?

Whom are you most like?

Whom do you most clearly and constantly show to the world?

You know what the answer would be if we were to ask that other Minister these three questions. And we are resting our whole theory of the ministry upon his. We are trying to get our ministry as close to his as we can. Somehow we seem to have set up a false difference between him and ourselves. Perhaps we did it in the interest of a doctrine or a reverence. Then let us hold fast what we have gained by that process and see what we can find in the way of identity between him and us. Some of his words scare us, because we could not possibly apply them to ourselves, though deep down in our hearts we are sure we ought to be able to do so. The chasm between Jesus and us is not so good a thing that we should exert ourselves either to preserve or deepen it. Not many ministries have been spoiled by being too much like his. The world has not had too many men like him in character and purpose.

Now, we know what he would say to these three questions. They would not sound commonplace or extravagant to him. I think they would seem to him to go to the very heart of his ministry, as they do to ours. Let us abandon all this hypothetical reasoning. Let us take the ifs and subjunctives out of our talk about Jesus. Repeat your questions, all three of them, to him, and every time the answer will be the same. Whom do you know best? God.

Whom are you most like? God. Whom are you trying to show to men? God. The words can be calmly written and quietly spoken, but they tell the story of the finest adventure of heaven and earth. What lies in them walks up and down through universal spaces, through life of God, through ministry of Jesus, and through humanity's wreck and its redemption.

Whom do you know best? The Bible is a book full of personal relations. Religion is a matter of personal relations much more than of personal opinions. The ministry is the most personal thing in the universe, the ministry of persons to persons with the chief Person as its center. If you were before a conference or a council, you would be asked what you know, and that would be well. And you might easily know one subject much better than others. You may have specialized or majored, as the modern term is, in history or Hebrew, in sociology or Greek. Such knowledge is imperative. Ignorance does not increase even a minister's efficiency. But there is a fundamental danger here. Teachers are not primarily teachers of subjects, even of advanced subjects. They are primarily teachers of persons. Preachers are not fundamentally specialists in subjects, but in personalities. Have you, therefore, specialized, or majored, in the God of our Lord Jesus Christ, so that you know him better than you know any other person or any subject at all? Or have you pushed the meaning out of all those rich personal terms there in the Bible, the terms those earlier men used? Do you think those earlier men, less carefully trained, were somewhat extravagant, or mystical, or figurative in these statements about their personal relations? Maybe they knew some one we do not know. Maybe our knowledge is thin where theirs was rich, and our lives shallow where theirs were deep and abundant. They said such things as this: "I know him." "I determined not to know anything but him." Have we a knowledge, an acquaintance that matches that? Or does it seem like religious extravagance to us, or the special privilege of men who lived in an earlier day? What would you say to this paragraph from a letter of Phillips Brooks, written in 1891? He was answering a young clergyman who had in all earnestness and sincerity asked the secret of his life. Among other things Brooks said: "All experience comes to be but more and more the pressure of his life on ours. It cannot come by one flash of light or one great convulsive event. It comes without haste and without rest in this perpetual living of our life. I cannot tell you how personal this grows to me. He is here. He knows me and I know him. It is no figure of speech. It is the realest thing in the world. And every day makes it realler. And one wonders with delight what it will grow to as the years go on." And what will you make of the story of Horace Bushnell? A friend one day said to him, "Doctor Bushnell, I think when the angel nearest the throne sees you coming he will say to the Master, 'There comes a man you know.'" And the great old man replied, "I trust so, and I am sure I shall know him." Why multiply words? Saint Paul, Phillips Brooks, and Horace Bushnell would hardly be called fanatics. It must be that they spoke the truth. You can ask any one of them whom he knew best and get that same answer. That gave them their right to speak to men. For, really, unless we and other ministers have this supreme acquaintance it does not matter much what else we have. Unless we know God in Christ better than we know any one else or anything else we are rattling brass and clanging cymbals. It does not answer just to know about Him. An acquaintance with a preposition like that in it is not personal enough for preaching purposes.

And take the second question: Whom are you most like? Whom do you most resemble in your character, your traits, your qualities,

your loves and hates, your moral features?
There is an old psalm that we always use at
funerals as if it were only good for dead men
to be buried with, when it is really one of the
best in the whole collection to live with. In
the older version there is a fascinating word at
the end of it—"Let the beauty of the Lord our
God be upon us." Think of having that happen to people like us! Of course we expect the
work of our hands to be established. There is
no mysticism in praying for that. That is just
good, hard practical sense. Even a minister
with a good business head, capable of being a
plain, infallible business man, could pray for a
thing as reasonable as that. But that other
prayer for the beauty of the Lord to be upon
us, that must be an extravagant figure of
speech. Some time, of course, if we are good,
we hope to "see the King in his beauty," but
to expect to have the beauty of the Lord upon
us, so that in us it might be seen, that is too
much for us. Of course we are now the sons of
God, but that means only the doctrinal, theological sons of God, or his sons for doctrinal
purposes. In some far future we shall be like
him, but, of course, not now. Let us be sen-
sible. Of course also "We all mirror the glory
of the Lord with face unveiled, and so are
being transformed into the same likeness as

himself, passing from one glory to another—
for this comes of the Lord of the Spirit"; but
this is a figure of speech, the sentence not
being easy to translate clearly, and must not
be forced to go on all fours. Nevertheless, as
"I hold this ministry, including this figure, by
God's mercy to me, I will not lose heart in it."
There are veils enough upon the hearts of people. We do not need to wear so many upon
our faces and characters. The beauty of the
Lord, if it is really upon us, need not be hidden
or dimmed like the lights on an automobile. If
you have it, the world will be glad, unless you
are self-conscious and proud about it. And
that will first conceal and then destroy it. If
you have it not, it does not matter much what
else you have. Unless you are more like him
than anyone else in the world—in character, in
qualities, in life, in spirit—it does not matter
much whom you are like.

A lad was asking a man about the father of
them both. The man was trying to tell the lad
what kind of man their father had been. He
piled up the noble adjectives, all of them true,
in the effort to make the boy see. It was
sorry and disappointing. It is not easy to con-
struct a personality out of adjectives or attributes. At last the lad broke in with this burning
question, "Are you like him?" And the older

one bowed his head and replied, "Friends tell me I am my father over again." And humanity is so full of younger brothers like this, like Philip. And humanity's way to God is so hard. It is so hard to get him clearly before the mind. You may pile up the adjectives, all of them true, but are you like him? Is his beauty upon you? Do you bear his image, so that your resemblance makes humanity's way to him easier and more sure? Do men find it easier to believe in God and understand him because they know you? Have you gone to the practical, personal depths or only to the homiletic depth of the words, "He that hath seen me"?

Whom, then, do you know best? Whom are you most like?

Finally, for to-day, whom do you most faithfully present to the world, to your world? Of whom do you or will you make your world aware in the deepest sense? This brings us straight to the question of the kind of God we know, the kind of God we are like, and the kind of God we shall preach. The difficulty is very great. It is very great for preaching. It is the double difficulty "of making a historic personality real" and making an invisible personality manifest. How can you see him? How can you show him? That is the local,

personal problem. It is the world problem as
well. The missionary problem at last is the
problem of making God real to the world. The
world's hunger and need are shown by the
gods and half gods it has created and set up.
Our problem is not the small problem of a God
for a small parish, but the problem of a God
for all mankind. The real struggle of Christianity is yet to come, not over. Christianity
cannot conquer unconquered India, China,
Japan, and Africa except with Christianity's
God, the God of Jesus Christ. I am speaking
all the time as a preacher, and as such I express
my conviction that for our purposes and uses
we do not come best to God through nature or
through man, but through Jesus Christ, for that
is the way he best came to us. Through acquaintance with Christ we come to know what
God is like. This is the method of knowing
him. This is the method of presenting him.
Too long, too much, has Jesus been regarded
and preached as though he were a protection
from God, rather than the revelation of God.
We have come to a good day for preaching, a
day in which we can preach the truth, that
God is Christlike. "He revealed perfectly because he was what he revealed." Henry Ward
Beecher had his gospel and his ministry saved
one day in his early manhood in Indiana by

the flashing discovery that he "did not need to believe anything about God that Jesus Christ had not taught and shown, and that he could believe and preach everything that Jesus Christ had revealed." There are gods that cannot be preached or understood either by preacher or hearer, but it renders a preacher simply imperial to be able to say out of personal acquaintance and personal resemblance, "God is like Jesus Christ." The glorious gospel of the blessed God in this way gets meaning and beauty and glory, gets into those regions where common men and women can lay hold of it. Personality is hard to understand and define, but a Person like this can be understood. It does not seem strange that such a God should meet all the ethical, religious, personal needs of men. Praying to such a God ceases to be vague and indefinite. Indeed, we can see how the impulse to ask for the things we ought to ask can easily come from such a Person. The personal terms in Old and New Testament become luminous when you think of knowing, of resembling, and of preaching such a God as this. Here is where Lord Tennyson must get his fresh vision. This is the quick, sure answer to the soldier in the trenches. This is the reply to the Japanese and American students. This is the word to the child, to the woman, to the man: "God is like Jesus Christ."

The foreign missionary movement has created a new problem, a kind of rivalry in deities. The next half century in which you will have your ministry will be full of amazing interest and importance because of this. If there were no other nearer occasion for it, we should be obliged to redefine our God for preaching purposes in view of what we must do in the non-Christian world where nothing can be taken for granted. And I do not hesitate to declare my glad conviction that God interpreted in the terms of the life and character of Jesus Christ is our sufficient disclosure both at home and abroad. Anywhere, in any land, in the presence of any other or all other gods, we can rest our case on the God of our Lord Jesus Christ. To know him is life eternal, to be like him is life transfigured, to preach him is life exalted and glorified. You do not fully know it, you young brethren, but you ought to be so glad to begin your preaching just now that together and alone you would sing a psalm of thanksgiving. Old heads are weary and old hearts are faint; the dust is on many lives and the hands of many hang down, but men with a God like this can renew the world in righteousness and beauty. The doctrine of the deity of Christ has not been pushed through to its full religious value. It has been a doctrine to expound, a theorem to demonstrate, a test of orthodoxy, a shibboleth to pronounce, but it has not been used for what it is worth in the religious life. But the "acknowledgment of God in Christ," as Browning puts it, lifts preaching far above the exposition of a doctrine. It brings us preachers into the fellowship of that other One upon whose preaching ours is based. He did not lecture about God to the trained and capable. He used what he knew of God in that perfect fashion that makes preaching a revelation. It made his preaching a delight. Modern preachers have been known to think more highly of Jesus Christ than of the God of Jesus Christ, to regard Jesus as more available and less difficult for preaching purposes. All this seems to me to be off the center. For us, as for him, the glory of our preaching is the God he revealed and declared. The God of Jesus Christ is not a pulpit embarrassment, nor a preaching difficulty. For Jesus and for us God was and is the strength, the warmth, the life of what he had and we have to say and show to men. His ministry was set far above all other because he had this God to reveal to men. Everything centers in that. He knew him, he was like him, he revealed him. That put him on the shining heights and in the life of the world. There can be no better thing for you. Of old it was believed that no one could see God and live. And a man in that olden time, after a night of wrestling, called a place Peniel, because he had seen God face to face and yet his life was preserved. We are in that better day which Jesus brought. Now we know that no one can live, no life can be preserved, without the vision of the face of God.

LECTURE II
THE MINISTRY OF REDEMPTION
"He shall save his people from their sins."

LECTURE II
THE MINISTRY OF REDEMPTION

THE subject for to-day is "The Ministry of Redemption." Anyone who prefers to speak of the ministry of salvation may do so without objection from me. We shall be thinking of the same thing and the same Person, and not be distracted by verbal refinements. Under either name lies untold wealth for the preacher, wealth that cannot be found anywhere else. This is emphatically the preacher's topic. We are thinking of the preacher, not the writer, nor the teacher, nor the administrator. For Christianity is a preacher's religion, because it is, above all things else, a religion of redemption and because a preacher can bring it directly to all human life.

I have no wish to conceal or delay making plain my purpose at this point. This subject contains the heart of what I am trying to say in all these days. The one word which I most desire to emphasize is the word "redemption"; the one Person whom I most eagerly desire to make clear is the redeeming God. We have taken the edge off of the redemptive idea in

Christianity, just as we have taken the redemptive glow from our conception of revelation. If that edge be gone or be dull, Christianity has no cutting edge left. God is not just a good, powerful, benevolent God, a God better than all the gods of the nations, a generally satisfactory God. The God of Jesus Christ is the God of the redemption of the life of mankind. Jesus Christ is the divine Saviour or Redeemer of men. The Bible is the record of the divine, redemptive movement in the world. The church is the society of redemption. In Christianity's view men and the world are the subjects of redemption. The ministry is the divinely appointed agency of redemption. Its message is the message of redemption. I put it all out thus, in full view, at the start, knowing that some will think it narrow and crass, fully aware of the reaction against a crude, raw evangelicalism, but fully believing that the redemptive note is the dominant note in the life and work of Jesus, and believing that nothing can save Christianity in its breadth and beauty, or make modern Christianity triumphant in the world, except a reemphasis of this note. Pardon these personal words, but I must interpret the ministry as it appears to me in the light of human need and Christ's purpose. I must make my testimony and leave my testimony,

that good ministers of Jesus Christ will be
ministers of redemption. For the preacher as
for Jesus, the center of revelation is not God
creating or ruling, but God redeeming. To this
dominant note other notes must conform. To
this end other conceptions must lead, and all
agencies and methods be adapted. From this
supreme purpose other purposes must follow.
My father, through many years, closed every
prayer at family altar or in public place, and
every blessing asked upon his simple meals,
with the words, "And this we ask for the dear
Redeemer's sake." With that tender memory
upon me I speak these words as he made his
prayers, "for the dear Redeemer's sake."

This conception of God as the God of redemption gives us a true center for the interpretation of the life and character of God. It
gives God preaching value, human value, rather
than simply theological or philosophical value.
With this in mind you can understand how the
redeeming God could and would become in-
carnate, and would at last submit to death on
the cross. The purpose of redemption on his
part explains his coming into and his methods
in the world. He revealed himself for redemption's sake. He spoke and acted, he lived and
died for the world. Many men have missed
the point of revelation both in its essence and

its purpose. Many have not seen beyond the revealing Redeemer to the God of redemption whom he came to reveal. Men have found it easier to preach the Saviour than to preach the Saviour's God, to preach Jesus Christ than the God of Jesus Christ. This ought not to be. God is the supreme value here, the supreme value to human life. And you can get him for preaching use by interpreting and knowing him as the God of redemption.

This conception gives us a true and working basis for the interpretation of the Bible, our chief book. The Bible has been for some years in tolerably bad plight. One after another, science, historical criticism, literary criticism, comparative religion have tended to disturb the traditional standing of the Bible. Preachers either shut their eyes and continued the old-fashioned use of it with wrath at the new forces, or swung clear over to the new basis with a brave show of faith which they did not feel, or got a clear vision of the real character of the Bible which set it in new strength and power for preaching purposes. It is and must be the preacher's book. With the Bible gone, or doubted, or discredited or misunderstood, preaching will always be in bad case. Now nobody wants anything except truth and reality here or anywhere; and nobody cares to save preaching for its own sake, but the human race is interested in the fate of the Scriptures and in the fate of preaching, because the race is interested in redemption. Maybe the race does not know it, but it is interested nevertheless, and vitally so.

Some thirty-five years ago a student of theology was in grave danger of losing both his personal faith and his possible message. He had been brought up on certain theories of the Bible which seemed no longer true, tenable, or valuable, and in letting them go he could not see how he could hold to the Bible itself. Many things seem to be real parts of our faith when actually they are only associated with it. In that crisis two influences came into that student's life. One of them was Phillips Brooks, the other Alexander Balmain Bruce. The first gave relief from a mechanical theory of the origin of the Bible by showing how it sprang out of life, the life of the redemptive God and the life of man whose redemption God sought. The other gave relief at a half dozen points by showing what is now a commonplace, that the contents of the Bible "chiefly relate to a purpose of grace, and its great watchword is redemption." The first answered the question how there came to be a Bible, the second what it supremely contained. Many mysteries remained and remain, but a living faith can exist in the face of some very perplexing mysteries. So for many years the Bible has been to that student a book of life and a book of redemption. Inspiration has been raised in importance by reason of its redemptive purpose.

If, now, you ask how there happens to be a Bible, and how it happens to be the kind of book it is, you can find an answer in the life out of which it came, the life of God in the world, the life of man in the world, though not the total life of either. For it is not a full history of the universe, nor a detailed history of humanity. The thing that lies behind it, that makes it what it is, is the movement of God in the world for man's redemption. This movement is the most important particular thing that has happened in our race. The literature that records and interprets it is for this reason the most important literature in the world. The movement gives existence, character, tone, and edge to the literature. Many things have tended through the centuries to take this emphasis off the literature. We shall deserve well of our own and other ages if we can make clear and sharp the church's sense of the Bible as the literature of redemption. It is not a literature which records a revelation of God in general, nor does it lay equal emphasis upon everything mentioned in its pages. It is chiefly, supremely, rapturously for us sinners, and gloriously for us preachers a record of the revelation of God as man's Redeemer and Saviour. The stream runs ever in one direction. The gropings and searchings of lost humanity after God make the finest chapters in human history, but this is not fundamentally that record. This is the divine story of the divine searching after men. Jesus does not appear as a discovery, but as a disclosure, a gift, a perfect word, a revelation of that seeking, saving God who is ever trying to redeem his children from evil and its destruction. The Bible is not, as Moulton has called it, above all things, an interesting literature. It is, above all things else, a redemptive literature. All its contents, all its characteristics, its inclusions and its omissions are conditioned by this supreme fact.

It contains lofty doctrines, it teaches noble ethics, it uses every good literary form, but in the heart of it "it is the record of redeeming love and purpose culminating in Jesus Christ." Mr. Henry James says in a lecture on Balzac: "The fault in the artist which amounts most completely to a failure of dignity is the absence of *saturation with his idea*. When saturation fails, no other real presence avails, as when, on the other hand, it operates, no failure of method

fatally interferes." There is no such absence of
"saturation with the idea" in the Bible. The
Book is full of its idea and was written because
of that idea. One night many years ago Wen-
dell Phillips delivered a magnificent oration,
magnificent even for him at his best. At its
close the editor of a powerful newspaper said to
him, "Mr. Phillips, I wish to publish this ad-
dress, and will do so if you will leave off the
last paragraph." And all the blue blood in the
orator's veins boiled as he answered: "Leave
off the last paragraph? I wrote the whole
speech just to say that." May we not say of
our Book, that the whole of it was written just
to show the person of the Redeemer and to say
the word Redemption? The great figure in it
is the figure of the Redeemer, the supreme word
the word of salvation, the holiest symbol the
cross, the living stream the river of the water
of life, life redeemed and perfected in Christ.
That was what Bruce said was the "Chief End
of Revelation." That must have been in Saint
Paul's thought when he wrote to the Corinthians: "I determined not to know anything
among you, save Jesus Christ, and him crucified." Think of writing that to the Corinthians
without even wondering whether they would
stand it or stand for it!

I quote three statements bearing upon this

matter. Dr. James Denney says: "The Bible has an infallibility not of information about everything, not even of historical accuracy, but of saving power. When a man submits his mind to the Spirit which is in it, it never misleads him about the way of salvation. It brings him infallibly to that knowledge of God in his judgment and mercy which is eternal life." The words of Robertson Smith are like unto these, and these words should have been remembered when other words were being used against him. "If I am asked why I receive the Scriptures as the Word of God and the only perfect rule of faith and life, I answer, with all the fathers of the Protestant Church, 'Because the Bible is the only record of the redeeming love of God, because in the Bible alone I find God drawing near to man in Christ Jesus and declaring to us in him his will for our salvation. And this record I know to be true by the witness of his spirit in my heart, whereby I am assured that none other than God himself is able to speak such words to my soul.' " Forsyth declares that the Bible is "not a history of Israel and the early Christians, it is the history of redemption." Milman long ago also said something like that.

You will see and will say that I am purposely avoiding such questions as inspiration, historicity, criticism, and inerrancy, and you will be correctly interpreting my attitude and purpose. I am thinking, as you know well, of preaching and not of anything else except as it relates to preaching. The questions of theology and of scholarship are not unimportant. The men who scorn these questions in the avowed name of piety and orthodoxy, who throw obloquy upon reverent men spending their lives in the determination of the truth concerning these subjects which are vital to life, serve neither piety nor orthodoxy. But we have in mind the men who bring to living congregations of men, women, and children not the processes of laboratory or the machinery of research but the message of life. What is the Bible to be, what can it be in the hands of such men, men in earnest, men eager to help, men with the spirit of that other Minister? Has the ministry of redemption any true, living message of redemption? And having lived through the storm and stress, the revolution and the quiet, the wisdom and the foolishness of the last thirty-five years, since these began to be real questions for me, I declare to you my testimony that this conception of the ministry as redemptive and of the Bible as the supreme literature of redemption sets the minister who holds it in a center of peace and power in which he can deliver his message of redemption and do the work of redemption, unfretted by the storms and clouds about him. The Bible is the record of how God came to men for their salvation. In its pages men can see the face of the Redeemer, by its light can find their way out of Egypt into Canaan, from the far country of husks and swine, to the Father's house. It is not a "repository of miscellaneous information on all sorts of subjects," but it is the record of how God was in Christ reconciling the world to himself, of how the Son of man came to seek and to save that which was lost. And that lifts it, for the preacher, above a lot of questions and renders it immune from a lot of dangers. Above all, it makes the Bible a preacher's book without any surrender of intellectual rights, or without requiring any reactionary, obscurantist attitude to modern learning. A score of questions will remain and be interesting, but in the midst of life the minister of life will have a word of life, and forever a gospel in the Gospels. And as he reads again and again this story of redemption the thing itself will grow upon the minister until redemption will appear to him the glorious thing it is. The book is so wonderful because redemption is so wonderful. It is not the small, petty task of saving a single soul from some sort of hell. It is saving a soul from death, saving it for life; saving a human race from death, saving a human race for life. This makes every feature of the movement magnificent. Redemption is God's own supreme achievement. He has done nothing else equal to this.

This conception also gives us a true and working basis for the preacher's understanding and interpretation of Jesus Christ. We get into the heart of our own ministry by getting into the heart of his. We preach not ourselves but Christ, and primarily Christ as Redeemer. Such mention as we may make of ourselves is of ourselves as redeemed by him. We are poor subjects for sermons, but very good subjects for redemption. Preaching Christ, as the familiar words run, is, after all, the only kind. And preaching Christ is not just preaching him in general, it is preaching him in the essence and heart of him and his work. He did not come, as we saw at first, to reveal just any sort of God. He came to reveal the God of redemption, the personal, saving God. He did not come just on a general mission of good will and service. He came on the holy errand of man's redemption. In the heart of him he was the Redeemer. In the simple but true lines of Dora Greenwell:

"He did not come to judge the world, he did not come to
     blame;
He did not only come to seek, it was to save he came.
And when we call him Saviour then we call him by his name."

64

Or, since we are quoting such lines, let us take these out of that old Bradbury hymn upon which a generation was brought up:

"There is no name so sweet on earth, no name so sweet in heaven,
The name before his wondrous birth to Christ the Saviour given."

Here, it seems to me, is the chief significance of Christ both for the minister's theology and his preaching. For all too many the chief interest has gathered about the Person of Christ as a doctrine, rather than about Christ himself as the Saviour from sin. Men are not saved by a doctrine, however true, nor by a phrase, however clear, nor by a proposition, however exact. Men are saved by a Person, only by a Person, and only by one Person. Preaching Christ has become a cant phrase, but it was first of all a true one. When now you define clearly the end of your preaching, the power of your preaching, and the way of your preaching; or when you define the way of it, the truth of it, and the life of it, you are compelled to do so in the terms of redemption and the Redeemer. The test of preaching comes most severely here, not at the point of the preacher's emphasis upon the deity of Jesus Christ as a doctrine, but at the point of his preaching of Jesus Christ as the Saviour. What is the end of preaching? It is

that men in sin and sorrow may be brought to
the Saviour from both. What is the power of
preaching? It is that the minister of Jesus
Christ has a Saviour who is able to save. What
is the way of preaching? It is the way of Jesus
himself, his way with fishermen, rulers of San-
hedrins, taxgatherers, and adulterous women, always the way of the Redeemer. Preaching is
not the exhibition of a doctrine. Even right
doctrinal preaching is not that. Preaching is
not the awakening of an emotion, though it will
do that. Preaching is not the wise showing of
the wise path to men seeking it, though it will
do that. Here is our human race, near and far,
in its sin, its ignorance, its weakness, and its
sorrow, and for that race, near and far, in your
small congregation and in the big world, the
problem of all problems is ever the problem of
the renewal of its life in righteousness, the
restoration of its life in moral character and
strength, the fortification of its life against
temptation and grief. And there is no other
name given under heaven or among men but
the name of Jesus. There never has been a
really great preacher who tried any other. And
there is no way to restore our ministry to such
power as it has lost except by setting again in
the very center of that ministry Jesus Christ
the Redeemer.

THE MINISTRY OF REDEMPTION

The chief end of revelation was redemption. The chief end of preaching is redemption. This is the center of Christian doctrine, the glory of Christian literature, the life of Christian ethics, the power of the Christian pulpit. Disaster and weakness have always followed Christian teaching and preaching when the chair and the pulpit, in teaching and preaching, have missed their proper emphasis. I know no way to save doctrine from its abstractness, literature from its emptiness, ethics from its impotence, the chair from its remoteness, the pulpit from its futility and littleness except by pouring again the stream of redemptive life into them all. I cannot wonder at Saint John's words. In old age he sits down to write his recollections, to put the gospel into his Gospel. He is feeble and aware of his own weakness, but not conscious of any other weakness than his own. The things his old eyes have seen, his old hands handled, when life was young, sweep before him like swelling tide or rising sun. And at the opening he writes, "In him was life." At the end he puts down, "Many other things Jesus did." He was not conscious of religion as a doctrine, or as an act, or as a law, but as a rich, new, abundant life in Jesus Christ. Here is the place for us to recover our power to make mighty affirmations free from ambiguity and uncertainty. Certain old authority is gone from the pulpit. New power is not yet born. The age is sensitive and uncertain at the very point where it should be neither. We cannot live, much less be omnipotent in this atmosphere. Nor can we regain our real authority by any effort to recover outworn doctrines. The authority of the pulpit does not lie in them and never did. The authority of the Bible over life lies in its redemptive depths. And we shall recover for the pulpit the only authority worth having when, reverently, obediently, we recover in our own ministry what made mighty men mighty—the life of God moving within and upon human life for its redemption. I can never hold again certain conceptions of authority and infallibility, but I can never lose again the vision of the Redeemer in the Word and the world.

Of course I know how easy it is to interpret redemption in a small, unworthy way and to make flippant remarks about getting people saved. I know all the cheap witticisms about insurance against fire in the next world and discomfort in this. I know how crass and narrow have been many of the ideas of the redeemed life, its imperfections, its lack of moral fiber and human sympathy. But there is a big view of redemption, a big view of individual redemption, and such a view of social and world redemption as makes life worth living even in troubled days. Maybe there will come a pulpit that will interpret the redeemed life as Jesus saw it. Maybe that pulpit will interpret that life in this large way to men, to races, and to nations. Maybe there will come a pulpit that will put the edge back upon the best truth we have, the truth of redemption. Redemption is very much more than a small revival in a small town, or the saving of one drunkard from his appetite, or one libertine from his lust, or the recovering of one sheep that has strayed, though that is enough to set the angels to singing. It is very much more than simply giving an individual a new emotion or a new sensation. The work of Jesus the Redeemer is no small thing even in an individual. We can only recover him for preaching purposes by recovering his own conception of his redemptive work in its fullness and largeness. You cannot make a great ministry, though you can secure immediate effectiveness, upon a small idea or truth. Some churches are winning large apparent success on very narrow ideas. Their zeal carries their thin edge far. It has always been a problem how to secure breadth of view and energy of spirit in the same person or group. It is for us to unite

theological competence with intensity of purpose. We must then interpret redemption and
the redeemed life in an adequate and worthy
way, if we are to be true and good ministers of
Jesus Christ.

What a glory it gives to preaching to have
Christ's conception of the redeemed life to proclaim. And what a strength and beauty, what
a life and power it gives to have such a Redeemer to preach to men and women. This is
the real good news. You have a lot of wonderful things to say, a lot of useful and valuable
things to teach, but you have nothing else half
so good as that message of redemption and
strength, salvation and comfort, which is the
gospel. Do not misunderstand the people before you next Sunday. Neither they nor you
are in a theological vacuum. They are not
wrestling against the principalities of doctrinal
refinement. Their interests are not academic
nor speculative. Really they do not care a
great deal about the age of the world or the
documentary hypothesis. They have been
beaten during the week by evil, they are being
beaten by it; the serpent that bites and poisons
is not a far-off fiction or figure to them. They
have a daily conflict to keep their lives clean
and their souls on top. More kinds of devil
are loose in the world than are dreamed of in

your experience. The people before you, and much more the people outside your four walls next Sunday, are having a constant warfare with all these hideous devils, the devils with the ugly, accurate names. "Now the works of the flesh are manifest, which are these: adultery, fornication, uncleanness, lasciviousness, idolatry, witchcraft, hatred, variance, emulations, wrath, strife, seditions, heresies, envyings, murders, drunkenness, revelings, and such like." Where you least suspect it often the battle is fiercest. It is not nice, of course. Leprosy is not nice in any form of it, whether you call it leprosy, lust, or licentiousness. I do not know what those demons were that got into people in the olden time, but I know what they did and what they do. For they still enter into the lives of people. You will come down from your Mount of Transfiguration after you have preached until you are in a rapture and find many a boy, beautiful, brave boys by the score, in the grasp of modern demons. Pippa, as she passes with her cheery song, ever goes by the men and women near to evil or in it.

And the sorrow of the world is as prevalent as its sin. Do not be misled by any false philosophy, no matter how brave or cheerful its words. Charles Sumner underwent the operation known as moxa. When asked if it hurt, he replied:

"Fire burns. I think there are not two opinions about that." In the youth of your ministry sorrow will not mean so much to you, but as you go on, walking by the world's graves, sitting in homes desolated by death or broken by disgrace and betrayal, you will know that sorrow is no fiction or fancy in the world of men. Of course men and women are brave. They do not give way nor whimper. You think time heals or causes them to forget, but do not misunderstand. There will be enough live sorrow in any congregation, small or large, to break the heart of an angel. Now, thank your stars, and bless your God, you preaching men, that in the presence of life like all of this you have a Saviour like Jesus Christ for preaching uses. And do not dull the edge of or withhold from constant pulpit use this very best truth you have. Sinning and suffering are desperately human. Never forget that men want to be assured about the seed of the woman that can bruise the serpent's head, that they cry aloud in their hearts for comfort, that they long to be fortified. Do not fail them. And do not mistake exhortations to righteousness for preaching Christ. You can lay down the law to men. You can declare what a great man called the glad tidings of damnation. You may call it preaching the gospel. But for preaching purposes righteousness of life is the promise of the gospel, and privilege in the Redeemer much more than a requirement of the law.

A thousand things can be preached around the Redeemer as the center, but there is no true preaching around any other center. For this is the heart of Christianity, Christ's personal presence in human life for salvation and friendship; salvation from sin, for character, service and friendship in the new life. Do not be so careful about the definitions of the redeemed life as to take the life out of it. And do not confuse knowledge of the processes with skill in securing the results. Here, as everywhere in our preaching, abstract terms are far less important than personal ones. Jesus is the Redeemer of men, of all men and of the whole of a man. Men may not know much psychology, they need not know much, to yield their lives to him for the rich experience that makes them over into new men. The transaction is personal like love. The power is personal in him, the result personal in the man. The man who is a sinner meets the man who is the Saviour, and the final outcome is a man who is a saint. And language fails us when we try to describe the thing. If ever Saint Paul loses his way in a paragraph, it is when he tries to tell what the Redeemer means to a man. His rhetoric runs riot, as if there were no restraining it, as, indeed, there is not.

And do not get mixed up about personal redemption, social redemption, and world redemption. There is a fundamental law that one good thing is not a substitute for another. Do not get foolish and go to decrying individual salvation while pleading for the salvation of society. Do not lose sight of a man's relations in life either while you go after the man himself. The word here, as in all preaching, is completeness, not election. We are always getting hold of one truth, or one phase of a truth, as though the part were greater than the whole. Jesus held things level, saw them steady and saw them whole. Redemption is individual. You cannot get ahead one inch except on that basis. The trouble with the world is its evil. Bad men, individual bad men, have to be made good men. The product is a Christian man, a saint in the process of development according to type, Jesus being the type. And redemption is social. Men live together, are members one of another. The outcome is a kingdom, in the process also, according to type, the New Jerusalem being the type, a kingdom of world proportions and extent. Back there a moment ago I read that ugly, hateful list of words which Paul used when writing to the

Galatians. It must have made him almost
sick to write them. He did not spin them off
in glee. Henry Drummond once said that after
a series of interviews with men about their
lives he felt he must take a moral bath. Saint
Paul knew what he was saying, and knew the
meaning of his awful words. And he goes
straight into a moral bath in the words that
follow. "But the fruit of the Spirit is love,
joy, peace, longsuffering, gentleness, goodness,
faith, meekness, temperance: against such
there is no law. And they that are Christ's
have crucified the flesh with the affections and
lusts."

This sounds like having put off the old man
and having put on the new. It sounds like one
of the descriptions of the redeemed life. There
are others just as good. But they all mean
character for the person and goodness in the
group. There is nothing small about it, and
nothing that cannot be preached with tremendous affirmations. There is nothing else
half so good for preaching. For the world has
failed at the point of character and broken
down at the point of relations. It has not
failed in wealth or intelligence, but in moral
character and moral relations. And you are
the preachers of the Redeemer of men in these
vital matters. Let nothing dull the edge of

your consciousness of your gospel as the gospel of redemption. Let nothing weaken your confidence in it. Many things do dull this consciousness. Beware of them. It is old, I know, but let no desire for false novelty, no sense of helplessness, no breadth of scholarship or sympathy rob you of the heart of your preaching message. It was said of Hugh Price Hughes that "he recovered for his church its ancient passion for the souls of men and set that passion in living power in the stream of modern life." There are men who have the ancient passion, others who are conscious of the stream of modern life. It is for you preaching men to be in that modern stream, not drifting with it, nor helpless before it, but with that ancient passion of redemption as an imperial power to make that stream a river of life like the one that flows from beneath the throne.

Christ as the Redeemer gives us our real message to the non-Christian lands, our missionary message, to be specific. We have no evangel to any person unless we have it for all persons. Our greatest need is not simply the need of the men and women in our town, it is the need of the men and women in our world, people like us on any planet that has people. Once the Jews sought after signs, the Greeks after wisdom. The Jews wanted evidence of

THE MINISTRY OF REDEMPTION

God's power, the Greeks light on the way of
life. Those early preachers offered in answer
Christ crucified, the power of God, and the
wisdom of God. Christianity then was young.
Its gospel had not become vague or uncertain,
elaborate and dull. It centered the power of
God and the wisdom of God in the moral
miracle of a redeemed, transformed life. It
laid far more stress upon making bad men
good than upon any other miracle. And from
Jacob to Jerry McAuley this is still the best
test near and far.

You may make the most of the good things
in other religions. You may make the most of
the beautiful characters to be found here and
there in non-Christian lands. Charles Cuthbert
Hall did that in fine and gracious spirit. Every
non-Christian religion has some good in it. Be
glad of it. Be glad whenever you find an excellence anywhere. There are some gold but-
tons on the garments of heathenism, flashes of
light in heathenism's darkness, lovely sayings
and radiant truths in its abysmal depths, beautiful characters in a dark world. But do not
draw a false inference from this. Heathenism
is not full of good people believing in bad or
mistaken religions, needing only to have their
religion changed. Many people have asked me
if the heathen world as I saw it is not getting

along pretty well with the religions it has. And
I wanted to find every good thing there was,
and rejoiced in every good thing that appeared.
But here is the answer: Nobody anywhere is
getting along pretty well without Jesus Christ.
The thing that burns into your very soul in
every heathen temple and before every heathen
shrine, and especially in the face of heathenism's life of sorrow and sin, is this: "There is
no other name." Humanity is morally wrecked,
and the non-Christian religions are helpless to
bring redemption. The whole race is sick unto
death, and there is no physician but One. The
problem of redemption for Jesus and for us
preachers is not the problem of a stray soul
here and there. It is the problem of a race
which has lost the way and with all its gropings
has not found it, a race in rebellion against the
law of life, a law it can break but not destroy.
Honestly, you come at last to wish that those
other religions were efficient for redemption,
they have such a hold upon such unthinkable
millions. But there is salvation in no other
than this. There is no other name, neither is
there salvation in any other. God was in
Christ and is in the world for man's redemption. That is the strength of your preaching
everywhere. Comparative religion does not
mean that Christianity is comparatively good,

but that it is absolutely good. No wonder the New Testament nearly bursts upon two subjects—the new Christ and the new life in Christ. The wineskins of language were tolerably tough and reliable, but they would not hold this turbulent new wine. And no man has any message to heathenism who cannot make mighty affirmations about this new life and preach tremendously this saving Christ. The cross he carried was not heavy because of the wood, but because of the world. Far past saving the Jews he had swept as he went up the low hill outside the gate. The ache of the world is not a thing of space or time or race. The movement for redemption stretches through the centuries and over the continents. It is not comfortable and complacent, shallow, local, or provincial. God is not at ease about this business here or anywhere. O, preaching men, good ministers of Jesus Christ, do you see what is yours to preach? Then into that wide-flowing, deep-running stream of modern life, into it with the ancient passion, the passion of Christ, the wisdom of God and power of God for man's redemption!

This conception also defines the church as the society of redemption. The Bible is the book of redemption, the Redeemer and the redeemed. Jesus Christ is the bringer of redemption. The church is the society of redemption. It has in it the Redeemer, the redeemed, and those who are being redeemed, and evermore it seeks to bring redemption near. The society of redemption, that is what it is on earth. The society of the redeemed, that it is and will be when its work is complete. There will be no statistics then; the great host will not be numbered, but there will be a song worth hearing.

Now, I am anxious all the time to keep the definiteness, the edge, the urgency of our message along with the breadth and largeness of the spirit which Christianity has created. The very intensity of early Christianity made inevitable, in course of time, a broader Christianity as its outcome. Then come two errors, one the denunciation of breadth, the other reliance upon it. You are to be preaching men, with churches. To you this is not an academic matter, but a very practical one. How can you preserve in a church that first zeal and intensity and not be a reactionary toward modern forces and conditions? How can you preserve intensity without narrowness, or passionate interest along with true breadth and freedom of spirit? Many men, feeling this difficulty, have broken with one or the other of these two ideals that really unite in their lower depths. The church itself has had long and genuine difficulty at this point.

THE MINISTRY OF REDEMPTION

The Young Men's Christian Association has had the same trouble—the trouble to preserve its first, best spirit and purpose along with its inevitable expansion and enlargement of activities and life. And I know no way for the church or any part of it except to hold fast to its redemptive purpose, to make itself a true society of redemption, and to permeate, to inspire, to inform all its activities with that original spirit. Redemption narrowly considered is fatal even to the redemptive movements. Activity, even the activity of a church, without the redemptive motive and power, breaks down for lack of that motive. The elder brother was busy at his father's work, but lacked the father's passion, the father's everlasting interest in the son who had gone away. The church has more than once been discredited and set aside because it has narrowly interpreted its redemptive mission. Other agencies have cut in behind the church, have set life flowing into other channels, have taken up tasks belonging to the church, tasks sometimes neglected by the church. The history is rather tragic in many of its features, lamentable failures lying all along the way. Nothing but a purpose to leaven the whole sad lump can save the redemptive leaven, nothing but the redemptive leaven can save the lump. There is no other force that will do it. The

church will lose what it has if it uses it in a small
and unworthy way. It can save its redemptive
leaven only by a true enlargement of its activity. But, on the other hand, there is no
salvation by any organization which is not a
society of redemption. Good it may do, splendid results it may accomplish; and some of
these valuable, secondary results may blind the
church as to its own character. It is easy to
misconceive the supreme purpose, easy to mis-
apply the final motive. The short view and the
near view often get in the way of the long, large
view. But, surely, the Church of Jesus Christ
the Redeemer, with the Bible, the book of redemption, in its hand, must ever be at its heart
the society of redemption. This will determine
its spirit. This will fix its standards of admission and its conditions of membership. This
will govern its activities, give tone to its preaching, its teaching, and its large total life. The
society of redemption will not assume an air
of superiority or exclusiveness in a world of men
fighting sin. It will be a modern city of refuge
for the hunted and hurt. And there will be
plenty of gates on each side of the city, so that
even a blind man can find his way in. Men
fleeing from any kind of wrath, present or to
come; men wanting safety against evil in any
form, will find it easier to find their way into

the society of redemption than anywhere else. The world is organized so that going wrong is easy, going right difficult. The society of redemption will reverse that order. At the risk of being misunderstood, but thinking of the Redeemer and the people who need him, I venture to say that Christ's society of redemption will fix its terms and its spirit so that it will be easy and desirable to get into it and hard and undesirable to get out of it, for it will not care to save itself; it will only care to save the lost. And so it will become all things to all men in the hope that in every one of these ways it may save some, through every one of these gates may induce many to come. And it will do all this for the sake of the good news of redemption, not that society may monopolize, but that it may share its benefits with all men.

This will not be simply the spirit that men who seek can find in the church, it will be the spirit the seeking church will everywhere show to men, the spirit men cannot fail to find. It will reveal the spirit of the Kingdom rather than the spirit of the ecclesiasticism. It will remember that it deals as a shepherd, after the pattern of the Good Shepherd, with all sorts of sheep, some old, some very young, some wandering, some not very valuable in the market, none very wise, but all infinitely better off in the fold with the shepherd than outside with the wolves. There is no room in this society of redemption for Pharisaism or spiritual pride, or personal assumption. There is no room for any spirit except the spirit of that Redeemer who is the ever-living head of the society.

I am not pleading for a narrow interpretation of the church, nor for a reactionary basis for its life. No narrow, reactionary church can live powerfully in this modern world. I am only pleading that the church devoted to reform, to philanthropy, to religious education, to social betterment, to industrial welfare and international peace, shall not lose its power in these good regions by forsaking or forgetting the basis and center of its power in the world. These are tremendous as allies, but deadly as substitutes for the gospel. The source of the church's power is its contact with the Redeemer, his spirit in its life, his purpose toward men in the world. The church of Jesus Christ must take its tone from the supreme purpose of Jesus Christ. Strong and useful it may be in many noble and beautiful ways, but it can only be a church of the Redeemer by being a society of redemption.

Three words have been spoken: the Bible is the book of redemption, Jesus Christ is the Redeemer, the church is the society of redemp-

tion. One more word remains: humanity is the
subject of redemption. Mankind in itself, in its
relations and in its conditions, all stands there
before the good ministers of Jesus Christ, in the
light of his life, his ministry, his spirit, his
cross, and his empty grave. His attitude must
determine yours. See that you do all things
according to the pattern shown in the mount.
His attitude will save you from taking a small,
meager, narrow, unworthy view of the meaning
and scope of redemption. His experience will
save you from the superficial view that the
task is easy and simple. His relations will save
you from race pride, class pride, wicked exclusiveness, national intolerance or ecclesiastical
assumption. His life will save you from personal complacency or professional ease in the
face of your task and his. It will save your
scholarship from barrenness and your intellectual life from death. Humanity as it is, humanity in its wrong and often frightful relations,
humanity in its conditions, its awful conditions
seen in the large, this humanity, seen through
the Redeemer's eyes, is the subject of redemption. For it he came, to it he came. For it he
lived, for it he died. To it he spoke, to it he
gave, always that it might be redeemed from
death to life eternal, from sin to goodness, from
destruction to salvation. Do not be too careful

to define- redemption. Remember what Coleridge said about making a truth too small by making it too definite. And of all truths this must have a large content, large in its reach into grace on one hand and into life on the other. It must never be slurred over as it must never be dropped out or allowed to get lost. How large this task is can be understood when you see it as he saw it. Let no man ever say that the ministry of redemption is a small ministry. All men in themselves, all men in their relations, all men in the conditions of their lives, were in the purpose of that other Minister. He could not speak to them simply as an orator or as a teacher. He must speak to them as a preacher whose object was their redemption. For their sakes he became poor, for their sakes he planted a cross in his life, for their sakes he was cast into the ground that he might not abide alone, for their sakes was lifted up that he might draw all men to himself. This is the great unselfishness, this the spirit of every true ministry, this the Golden Rule of the higher life, this the magnificent adventure. You can go either one of two ways in the world and in the ministry, but you can go only one way with him. You can go the way of saving yourselves, or you can go the way of saving humanity. This latter way leads through Nazareths, Capernaums, Gethsemanes, and Calvaries, and is lined with fishermen, lepers, Magdalens, publicans, thieves, and the like. But out of this soiled and motley crowd come those who walk in this way after him, drawn by his Spirit, thrilled by his presence, obedient to his word. They wear white robes, they live in love, they sing a new song, they are new creatures. And they are a host that no man can number.

LECTURE III

THE MINISTRY OF INCARNATION

"The Word was made flesh, and dwelt among us."

LECTURE III

THE MINISTRY OF INCARNATION

A THOUGHTFUL person can hardly help regretting that such mystifying and appalling names have got themselves attached to certain matters of deep interest and common concern. The names given to diseases add to the terror of being sick. The shadow of the name overcomes the patient. The religious value of many doctrines is greatly modified by the terms designating them. It is rather a fearsome experience for the average congregation when these terms, perfectly proper in their place, get loose in a sermon. An ordinary saint is not sure he wants to be saved when he hears the theological name for salvation, or live forever when he hears the theological term for the doctrine of the future life. And it seems a real misfortune that so human, warm, personal a truth as the truth of the incarnation should have had to bear a name so distinctly difficult. The very mention of it usually sets all the bristles of debate into action, whereas actually there is not a word in our language with more love and grace and good will in it. But it is not a good word for preaching purposes, except perhaps in very select circles. We are concerned about the preaching value of supreme truths, and we are anxious that the inevitable names belonging to them shall not destroy this preaching value. We do not want to lose the truths or have them obscured. Our concern is with people and with preaching to them, and we must use truth for that purpose. This is not a low or common ideal. It does not cheapen learning to popularize it in legitimate ways. Science is glorified and exalted when it is pressed down into the folds of the common life of the world. When the science of chemistry improves the daily food of men, chemistry is exalted. Ore must be minted in order to its circulation as currency. The preacher is to do this with truth, fit it for use by common men, like gold coin or wholesome food. The philosopher and the scholar have great and significant use in the preacher's world, but it is for the preacher to interpret, to translate into the familiar speech of man what otherwise will be in an unknown tongue, true enough but not understood. The preacher uses the leaven of learning to leaven the mass of unleavened life which will be inexpressibly sad without it. I beg you, therefore, to cure yourselves early of that conceit which despises the right sort of popular preaching. If you have not the kind of speech that common people love to hear, do not be proud of it or think yourself a superior person because you lack it. Remember whose company you are not in when the common people do not hear you gladly. And His company we principally covet.

Now, after all that, I am obliged to say that the good minister of Jesus Christ will have a ministry of incarnation, as he will have a ministry of revelation. Incarnation will be the way he will accomplish his ministry of revelation for the purpose of redemption. But having said it, we can hurry at once into the personal warmth, the human feeling and divine glow of it, which will be good for our souls and good for our preaching.

How fine a thing it is for a man to interpret his vocation or profession as that calling appears in the life of the best person in it! A teacher may be very obscure and unknown, a very insignificant member of his noble profession, but all teaching is glorified for him by the life of Thomas Arnold. The medical profession is distinguished for all doctors by such physicians as William MacLure. I can recall across more than a generation of years the new way the ministry looked to us in our youth when we heard Phillips Brooks preach. It was not vanity, it certainly was not any feeling that we could ever do it as well, that led us, after hearing him, to say with a kind of exaltation, "I also am a minister." Interpreting the high calling in the light of this man in it, the ministry in the terms of this minister, made it seem a vastly higher and finer calling than it had seemed before. And this seems good yet. Our impressions and convictions concerning our lives must always be shaped and formed by these best examples. We must always have the sense of kinship with the best. As Emerson says in the essay on History: "All that Shakespeare says of the king, yonder slip of a boy that reads in the corner feels to be true of himself." But see where all this swiftly and surely leads us. We cannot stop short of the most perfect Person who ever trod these ways. Our ministry, we ourselves as ministers, must finally be interpreted in the light of his life and ministry. We must be and must feel ourselves to be kin to him. He must not be inexplicable to us. We must be able to unite him to ourselves and reconcile him to our aspirations. We cannot forget his perfections and the vast, vital differences between us, but neither can we forget the vast, vital relationships between him and us. And evermore a holy ministry will find Christ's ministry, his words, his deeds, his spirit luminous and significant to it.

And now I want to try to get into the incarnation, not in its theological aspects, not as a doctrinal shibboleth, not as a test of orthodoxy, but in such fashion as will really relate it to our ministry and relate our ministry to it. It must be an object of study and interpretation. It must also be an object of practice and imitation. The good minister of Jesus Christ must base the spirit and method of his ministry on the spirit and method of Jesus Christ's earthly life and service. The Master and the men must have the same principles. With every allowance for what is different, the modern ministry can only be saved by its essential resemblances to that early and perfect ministry. And the modern ministry needs to be saved all the time from a lot of things, such as low ideals, officialism, professionalism, commercialism, and discouragement. The ministry tends ever to be conformed to the world around it rather than to be transformed by the renewing of its mind. It is always tempted to shape its message by what the people will stand rather than to speak the word of Christ. Or when it does get what it believes to be the prophetic or apostolic spirit, it is ever in danger of becoming denunciatory and reckless, mistaking violent speech for true speech, and a needless, self-imposed dramatic public martyrdom for fidelity and courage. The ways of the enemy of our ministerial souls are very subtle. He has immense skill in destroying us. I sometimes think he has special pleasure in causing a modern minister to think himself a prophet to his generation. The true prophets of a generation are the salt of the earth, but once a prophet in modern days becomes self-conscious he quickly loses his savor. The cure for all this partial and imperfect ministry lies in having Christ formed in us, being made complete in him. He belonged neither to an age nor to a type. And likeness to him is a remedy for religious exaggeration on one hand and underdevelopment on the other. Archbishop Temple used these words: "If I did not believe that Christ had by his incarnation raised my whole life to an entirely higher level—to a level with his own—I hardly know how I should live at all." Saint Paul used even stronger words: "To me to live is Christ"; and, again, "Christ liveth in me." That saves our manhood and our ministry, as it saved Saint Paul's.

But, now, how can you put the matter of the incarnation in current terms, terms free from technicality and scholasticism? How can you make it clear that the way of incarnation was the best way, possibly the only way, the redemptive God could reveal himself to men, and get himself into human life for the purpose of redemption? He must make his revelation through and in a personality and get his contact with unsaved persons by a saving Person. For remember that we have to make these deep things as clear as possible to men and women who do not pretend to be theologically competent. The men and women whose redemption we seek are always before us. I dislike to speak of the man on the street or the average man, because talk about these well-known persons has been rather overdone. But let me give you this experience with a man of another class. After one of the student conferences a devout, earnest, recent graduate came to one who had spoken two or three times to the conference, with this frank statement: "I am an orthodox but perplexed member of an orthodox evangelical church. I believe in the incarnation, but am in an utter haze about it and cannot seem to get through to any clear view that will satisfy me. I am not a skeptic. I do not care to argue, but I wish you or some one would put this matter so it would mean something vital to me. It ought to mean more to me than it does or else it ought not to mean so much. Somehow I have not got it into my life as a real and significant force which corresponds with its place in my creed." Now, what would you say, on a railroad train, to an earnest young Christian scholar in that state of mind?

Of course you could smile at the immaturity of it. You could be superior and scholarly. You might even wonder where such a person had studied. You might even quote your favorite lecturer, using or omitting the quotation marks. You might argue as with a budding heretic. And you could easily lose your chance to guide a life aright. For while you were doing all these things the man might easily escape. What did that older preacher do and say? He is not much of a scholar. His learning is not very modern, and it never was technical. But his spirit he has tried to keep modern, and his attitude to life he tries to keep human. He never sees a young man like that perplexed graduate without having a thrill which he humbly thinks must be akin to the feeling Jesus had when he saw the rich young ruler and loved him. What, then, did he say to this youth? He asked a few simple questions in the spirit of a pastor: "Would it seem strange to you that a strong man should put himself into the very life of weak men to help them, should take their very weakness upon himself, to save them from their weakness? Would it seem strange to you that a learned man should go with his truth and learning into the very lives of people ignorant and in bondage, should take the very limitations of their lives upon him, to

98

set them free? Would it seem strange to you that a good man, a holy man, should take his goodness into the heart of evil, should take men's evil upon himself that he might destroy it and deliver them from it? Would it seem strange to you that a rich man should go with his wealth into the midst of poverty, should become poor that others should be rich, that one holding health in his hands should go into any kind of plague, even at the risk and cost of his own life, that he might heal the sick and banish disease?" They were simple questions, perhaps they seem very commonplace, but the youth laid hold of them. He was recently from college and spoke its language. Reverently but rapturously he replied after a moment: "Is it like that? If you put it that way, I do not see how God could keep out of it. He had to get into it just because he is God. And he had to get into it that way because that was the only way. He had to do it, he could do it and he did do it." Then there was a silence. Then shortly, with the frank logic of youth, that modern disciple added, quietly: "I do not see how I can keep out of it either. I guess I can clear up the thing by doing it."

And that preacher, no longer young, sat there thinking of that other ministry and of his own, and the ministry of his brethren. The incarna-

tion did not seem to be an isolated event, a
solitary experience for one person, a closed
chapter in religious life. Always the unique-
ness of the Master's experience was before him,
but no longer did that experience seem solitary
and unrelated, though always the supreme fact
in history. Nor did it seem chiefly a matter of
metaphysics, but chiefly a matter of personal
life, purpose, and power. It seemed ethical,
vital, and religious, and because of the unique-
ness of that earlier experience it seemed and
seems to be a process, a principle, and not
simply an event. Surely, so living, so necessary,
so beautiful a thing was not exhausted in one
life, however perfect. Surely, what so glorified
his ministry ought not to be lacking in ours.
If our ministry is to be based upon his, if we
are to be good ministers of Jesus Christ, must
not this mind be in us also? And where can we
get it except where he got it? How can we get
it and keep it except as he got it and kept it?
We can neither get away from him nor get on
without him. We must not identify the super-
natural with the abnormal and the impossible.
The experiences of Jesus must all be viewed in
the light of his oft-used words, "The kingdom
of heaven is like." He was not less related to
men than to God, not more a revelation of one
than the other. If you ask what God is like,

the answer is, "Jesus Christ." So if we ask
what is real humanity, we look at Christ to
find the answer. No one sentence from him or
his Book fully covers the case for us. A dozen
sentences arise out of the New Testament
charged with this rich meaning. The atmosphere of the Gospels envelops us with it. Take
that immortal utterance standing up there in
the very opening of John's Gospel—"The Word
became flesh." Of course we all know what the
original Greek term is, and of course also we
are not going to be pedantic here or hereafter
and make cheap criticism of the translation, or
vain references to the original. That is too
obvious and vulgar to be impressive anywhere.
It is not a display of scholarship, which should
never be displayed, but of foolishness which
ought always to be kept concealed if possible.
But the best kind of exposition in this world is
the kind that takes a familiar word or text and
by proper paraphrase and use of other words
makes the familiar fresh and luminous, so that
the uneducated rejoice as those who have seen
a vision. For example, the incarnation in spite
of its name is not chiefly a thing of the flesh,
but a thing of the person. Suppose, then, as a
sort of commentary on the statement of John,
for ourselves and for others, we should make it
read as one of the later paraphrases does: "And

101

the Word became a Person. The Person dwelt
with other persons. The Person was full of
grace. The Person was full of truth. The
Person was full of reality. And other persons
saw his glory, saw it at close range, walking
around among them, making a new kind of
Person visible. And they knew where he got
his glory, and little by little the life of this
Person became the light of other persons."
That sounds as if it might be the biography of
a "Sky Pilot" or the story of a "Singular Life."
The Word of God became a man, the message
became a living epistle, a real letter, a true
letter, a love letter. And other men read and
knew where it came from and where it got
those qualities. Incarnation does not appear to
be some far off, individual, isolated, closed event
in the light of such words as these. Maybe
under this influence, some day, "Such a man as
this will arise in me and the man I am will
cease to be."

One day that other Minister went into the
village church at Nazareth, his home town,
where he had been brought up. It was not a
town to be proud of. If you came from such a
place, you probably tell strangers you came
from near New Haven or some other such place,
half way between Albany and Boston. That
village church was probably about as uninter-

esting as any modern church in any small town.
The people, to quote the late Dr. Storrs, were
doubtless "dull and respectable" and doubtless
"respectable and dull." You will think yourself buried when you become pastor of such a
church. A call to one will hardly seem provi-
dential; an appointment to such a church will
be regarded as just ground for denouncing the
episcopacy as an invention of the devil. When
a bishop sends a recent graduate to such a town
as Nazareth it is quite proper to call the bishop
a prelate and to rebel against ecclesiastical authority and officialism, against a system that
makes such things possible. But that other
One went to Nazareth one day and went into
the local meetinghouse. Let your imagination
play upon the scene. You will meet it all. It
was what we call an ordinary congregation. It
did not expect any mighty thing to happen.
Such congregations never do, nor do ministers
to such congregations. Anyhow, the people did
not expect it to happen right there in their
town before their eyes with one of their own
neighbor's sons. Somebody handed him the roll
of the old prophet. He opened to certain familiar words, words that had once been full of
life, words that had become a dead letter. The
priests could drone those words out without
waking anybody from his Sabbath sleep, or

quickening anyone's pulse rate. You can do it now. You can take all the emphasis off the personal terms and every bit of color out of the immortal sentences. Or you can do a worse thing still, the worst thing going on in the modern ministry: you can utterly detach yourself from your message so that it will have small meaning for you or anyone because it has small meaning in you. You can take a word of Christ as though it had meaning only for him and none at all for you. That is one way dead letters are made. Literature comes from life and lives only in life.

Now, that other young Minister took that dead letter up into his living hands and all at once it began to breathe and glow and live there in that old synagogue. He put the emphasis where it belonged, upon the personal terms and personal relations: "The Spirit of the Lord is upon me," he said, and no one doubted upon whom it was. "Because he hath anointed me," he went on, while the heavens opened upon a man touched by God's own touch. "To give all sorts of mankind, deaf, blind, imprisoned, poor, a chance," he continued until the walls fell down and all the human helplessness and need in the world were right there where the Spirit of the Lord was falling on a man. God was getting into it, as

the student said on the train. Then this young
Nazarene said, quietly and confidently: "This
day is this scripture fulfilled." This written
word is become a living word, this printed thing
has become a personal thing and is going to
walk around into the jails, the asylums, and
the slums. And at such low ebb were expectation and faith in that congregation that the
people wondered and shook their heads and
began to talk about his folks. They no more
expected such things to happen to a man from
Nazareth than the usual congregation would expect it to happen to a man from the theological
seminary. A display of scholarship, or even
foolishness, they might look for, but for nothing
like this. But there are moods, moods which
ought to be constant, in which a minister cannot read that story with composure. Who was
he, and who are we, that that thing which happened to him should not happen to us? What
chance is humanity going to get unless the
Spirit does fall upon us as it did upon him?
Centuries and countries have nothing to do with
it. "The wind always bloweth where it listeth
and maketh kin of holy souls." Still upon us,
as upon him, the Spirit of the Lord must
fall if we are to proclaim any acceptable
years of the Lord, if we are to heal any broken
hearted, if we are to open any blind eyes or deaf

ears. Everything in any ministry depends upon that.

Did you ever think what you would have done if you had been sitting in the synagogue that day, or can you now imagine what you would do if all at once the essential scene should be repeated right here in this chapel? Of course you are not "dull and respectable" like that older group. You would do something besides rub your eyes and make empty remarks about Joseph's family. But if you were like many modern congregations, you would be likely to fear some new fanaticism, some serious disturbance of the sanctified social order, and conclude that you would better wait and see how he turns out, whether he is going to be safe or not. But even reading the story, across the years, there are men, some of them no longer young, who feel in their bones that if they had been in that older group they would have scandalized the orderly proceedings by leaping to their feet, waving their caps, and crying out loyally to that other One, "We are with you; if that is the Spirit and the program, we are with you." It would not have been prudent, nor conventional; it would have offended the standing order, but many of us have shouted ourselves hoarse for far less cause. And I would feel a lot better about our ministry if this sort of thing were more universal in it, or if our response to this experience and our sense of kinship with the central figure in it were altogether universal. He is the point of contact between divine power, the Spirit of the Lord, and all human need. In him the Spirit gets a chance to serve, and humanity a chance to be saved. Really I know no better conception of a true ministry than that. It is not reverence to set this case apart; it is both wisdom and reverence to get ourselves as far into it as we can. This is the true ordination both as to source and purpose.

We are thinking of the incarnation, in its practical personal phases, thinking of our ministry in the terms and experiences of the Master's, never forgetting his unique place and character. And the record is so rich, for our special purposes, that we hardly know what to take and what to leave. When we read the record with this in mind we are amazed at its fullness and suggestiveness. Take that simple story told by Peter in the house of Cornelius, "how God anointed Jesus of Nazareth with the Holy Spirit and with power"; and how he "went about doing good," and curing all who were under the power of the devil, because "God was with him." That sounds like a description of a minister's work or a missionary's. Indeed, there is a story from the mission field that breaks right in at this point. There was an English missionary in India who always had trouble with his accounts and finances. He was not at all a capable business man. He spent all his money for missionary work, but not according to the plans. He got his accounts mixed and could not balance his books. And, of course, that could not be endured. Unless a missionary or a minister is capable of double-entry bookkeeping he has no capacity at all except for mischief. So many seem to think. Many congregations would apparently rather have a business man's administration than to have a true prophet in their pulpit. This poor missionary was dismissed as being unfit for missionary work, whereas he was only unfit for bookkeeping. He went off alone to a section where he would not be bothered by accounts. "Several years later a woman was visiting a distant village in the jungle. She tried to make the simple village folk understand what manner of person Jesus of Nazareth was. She told them how he was the poor man's friend, how he used to eat with them and visit their homes, how he used to go about healing wherever there was sickness, how the children used to run after him in the street and clamber about his knees. Her description seemed to meet with an unusually intelligent response; and as she finished some one exclaimed, 'Miss Sahib, we know him well; he has been living here for years!' Amazed, the woman discovered that this missionary had settled there on his own account. It was he who fetched the old men and women their water and their food. Where anyone was sick it was he who would sit outside the door until evening and then come in to watch through the night. When plague and cholera visited the village he was the intrepid nurse. In the old man who could not keep books the people of that village had seen and recognized Jesus Christ" (Robinson: The Interpretation of the Character of Christ, pages 21, 22).

Would anyone hearing a simple description of the daily activities and spirit of Jesus be reminded of you, do you think? Would anybody say, hearing such description, "We know him well; he has been living here for years"? Have we stressed the miracles Jesus performed until we have come to think of him chiefly as a miracle-worker? Have we failed to see that the most significant thing is not the occasional, extraordinary deed, but the constant kindness and beauty and spirit of his life? He did not go around doing wonders all the time, but he did go about doing good all the time, and that was a wonder in his world. Because we cannot repeat his miracles we are inclined to think we cannot repeat his life at all. But the power to work a miracle would not be nearly so useful a power to put into our hands as the power to go about doing good, which is put into them. The power to multiply loaves and fishes in an emergency is good, but the spirit that refused to make bread for himself, to use his power for his own benefit, and did make bread for others, did use power in their behalf, is the real value. And that spirit is for us as for him. If it be not in us, then he has no ministry left in the world. We stand in awe before the cross, as we ought, but we ought to understand it perfectly from our own attitude and spirit. It ought not to be a blind mystery to us. We ought to know what it means to save others and not ourselves. The incarnation is a blank perplexity to a man or a minister who comes to be ministered unto and not to minister to the point of giving his very life.

Why do we get the whole business of the imitation of Christ off its feet? Why do so many think they exalt him when they only remove him? There used to be a test of orthodoxy as to the inspiration of the Bible, to the effect that it differed from all other inspiration, not only in degree, but in kind, as though the

farther away we could get it the diviner it
would be. Surely, we know better than that
now. Life is not helped by its distance from
Jesus, but by its nearness to him and his nearness to it. The operations of the Spirit, the
experiences that were good in his life must be
good in ours. Kindness is not one thing in him
and something else in us. His deeds were not
done that they might have a homiletic or apologetic value. They were not chiefly evidences,
but examples, not chiefly for sermonic use, but
for daily use. Our interest is not professional
alone, but personal.

What has been said about his deeds applies
equally to his speech. What are the two favorite
texts about his utterances? "Never man spake
like this man," is one, and the other is, "The
common people heard him gladly." And these
two sentences are used to prove that by the
character of his speech Jesus showed himself to
be divine. And we compare his utterances with
the sayings of other religious masters, to show
how superior his are. We usually speak of their
originality, their depth, and their disclosures.
Now, of course, no one else ever had spoken as
he did, and no wonder the mass of the people
heard him with delight. It was the world's
tragedy that no one had ever spoken to men as
Jesus did, that no one had ever brought them

such good news as he brought them. It is
enough to make us weep to read how in Nazareth's synagogue those old saints wondered at
the gracious words he said. To such a pass
religious speech had come that such words as
he spoke, such gracious words, such hopeful
words, such loving words, amazed them. And
to such a pass had caste and a false privilege in
religion come that the masses got their first
delighted chance at life in Jesus's words. No
wonder they heard him gladly. Poor John the
Baptist lost heart, got clear down into the
depths about religion, when he was in prison.
You remember how Jesus cheered him up. Go
back and tell John, he said, that I am doing
good deeds and telling good news to everybody.
We forget the difference between that year and
this, and we vainly try to make out that the
common people heard him with such delight
because of the way he spoke, because of his
oratory and rhetoric. And then we go silly in
our effort to talk simply, to talk down to the
common people. But the common people heard
him with such delight, heard him as India's
outcasts do to-day, not because he used words
of one syllable, or used his voice with an orator's
skill, but because he opened the straight and
shining way of hope and life, of love and liberty,
to men, men who had been crushed and hope-

less for a thousand years. It was amazing then because they had never heard or seen it on this wise before. In a land familiar with the hard, inhuman lines of caste, or special privilege sanctioned by religion, buttressed by ecclesiastical authority, and, as men thought, approved by God himself, a message like the message of Jesus turns the world upside down and right side up. It amazed, perplexed, and enraged the privileged classes then as it does now. It stirred new depths in those who never had had a word of hope and privilege spoken to them. It was wonderful then, but after nineteen centuries there ought to be a whole Christian ministry speaking as he spoke. And instead of anybody being surprised when the common people hear a minister gladly now, there ought to be amazement if a minister speaks so that they are not glad. The tendencies, religious and social, that had hardened into the conditions that Jesus met are just as present to-day as they were during the centuries before he came. The caste system is not confined to India. Our ministry is to our age and its conditions just as the ministry of Jesus was to every age. He won the praise of the officers, he awoke the rapture of the multitudes, not by the originality, nor the scholastic profundity, nor the eloquence with which he spoke, but by that gospel of God which he spoke in love, love for the message and love for those to whom he spoke it. The democracy of that gospel is not given to it by popular vote. It is democratic because it is from God, the Father of us all. We go far astray when we praise the superior speech of our Master and rhapsodize over the way that speech was received, as though he and it stood far apart from us and our speech. Our praise of him is of small value unless we have caught, not the externals of his speech, but the spirit behind it and in it. It is small matter what we say or how we say it if our speech and our preaching are not in the same spirit as were his.

This is a very different thing from so-called popular preaching, which some despise and others affect. There is nothing more pitiable than an unpopular preacher, except a popular preacher who has won popularity by the ways of the demagogue. Many a man gets a tremendous hearing for everything except the gospel of Jesus Christ. Some affect indifference to popular favor, declaring that they will speak the truth whether men will hear or whether they will forbear. But for a minister of Jesus Christ there is no popularity worth having except the kind he had, won as his was won. And there is no opposition to be proud of except such as he suffered and for like causes. Both

popular favor and popular opposition may come
to us on un-Christlike grounds. They turn to
bitterness before the end of the day comes. All
this seems so far from those rich words about
our Master: "Never man spake like this man."
"The common people heard him gladly." It
was not because he was orator or agitator, but
because he said the things best worth saying to
men, and said them as well as they could be
said. What he said and how he said it were
both of a piece with all the rest of his life and
character.

Do you propose to speak as no one else does
in your town? Do you propose to speak so
that people will hear you with something of this
ancient delight? Who else should speak as you
do? Who else has such a message as yours?
Who else has such a motive and purpose behind
him as you? Who else has such subject and
such object as yours? Who, so much as you,
cares alike for truth and people, so that you
will not speak falsely and will not speak indifferently or academically? Who in this world
comes by his speech into such a fellowship as
the fellowship you have with that other One
in striking all the chords of human life with the
magic power of Christlike speech? Nothing
takes its place, nothing rivals it. Woe to the
man who regards it lightly, uses it carelessly, or

treats it indifferently. We are a speaking people, particularly a speaking profession. If it was important that holy men in olden time should be moved by the Holy Spirit before they spoke and as they spoke, it is important still, even more important now than then. That Christ should have spoken in his wonderful way, that men near him should have done it, must not be regarded simply as miracles on which we can look back. We speaking men can only be saved from being sounding brass and tinkling cymbals by the presence in us of that divine power which made their speech effective and gracious and which alone can make ours effective and gracious. The marvelous thing about the speech of Jesus was the temper, the tone, the spirit of it. If by papal decree this could be assured, it would be far better than the infallibility so much prized. But by contact with Jesus in the Holy Spirit the temper, the tone, the Spirit that made his speech what it was can be had. Nay, it must be had. What response, then, do you make to these and many other words spoken there in the brief history of that other Minister's life? Your opinions on many subjects are important, but your attitude to this is crucial.

It is only saying the same thing in slightly different fashion when we say that your personal reaction to the experiences of Jesus constitutes just as severe a test. How does your life respond to his? We are always looking and sometimes praying for light upon our problems. We are not quite so careful to acknowledge that the light in us has become darkness. Really, we do not need to pray for any more light upon certain problems. Our lack is the lack of light within ourselves. The life that was in him has not become light within us. We praise it as some divine, bright, shining thing far off yonder in time and space, a personal wonder that once surely was. But we do not respond to it as "a life able to repeat itself—able to generate life in those who give it opportunity and room." We gladly acknowledge the marvelous in him—that is our orthodoxy. We do not expect within ourselves the marvelous from him—that is our unbelief. His incarnation as revealing a type of personality never before seen, never since seen, we put at the center of the creed. We are not so swift to recognize in him a power to operate upon other men, to touch them to new issues, to tune them to divine pitch, to transform them into the same image. We regard his incarnation as a revelation, as it surely is. But it is more. It is creative and dynamic. That such a personality should have appeared at all is a wonder until you learn what God is like. That it should have appeared without any power to reproduce itself in other personalities would be a blind wonder. He would not mock us with mere words, or baffle us with a dazzling but impossible ideal. His commandments and promises were all with power.

I am thinking all the time, you see, of our ministry in the light of his. And just now we are forced to think of our personalities in the light of his. This, after all, is what incarnation means, for the earliest question about the ministry is the question of the minister. We cannot interpret our calling in terms of law, or of doctrine, in terms of ecclesiasticism or in terms of orders. We can only do it in the terms of personality. James Martineau once said, "Jesus Christ shows us in living definition what the Christian ought to be." Make all the objection you wish to that statement, for our purposes it contains the supreme thing in this realm. Perhaps the ministry has no larger philosophical task than the recovery of the world from its mad departure from the high truth of personalism. The universe is being thought of in terms of law and in terms of matter, or in terms of force. The chemist is a prisoner in his own laboratory. The supreme thing is the laws and not the man. We have come to explain miracles, the miracles of Jesus, by showing how they could have happened or could have seemed to happen, without destroying the sacred laws of the material universe. Now, as ministers we are greatly interested in a regular order, a world in which sun and seasons can be relied upon. A capricious universe would be utterly intolerable. But our world is not chiefly the world of matter or of material law, but the world of men and women, of children growing to youth, of youth growing to maturity; the world of free, tempted, struggling persons; the world of wise, foolish, good, bad, partly good, partly bad persons; the world of a free personal God, free in his universe; the world into which Jesus Christ came showing what personality truly is; the world of a personal ministry with personal character, and personal relations toward God and men. No other occupation of men—not teaching, not medicine, not law, not anything—is more personal or more dependent upon personality than is the ministry. Its immediate goal is the making of saints, who are really persons like Jesus Christ. Its method is personal chiefly and not chiefly institutional. Its reliance is upon personality, its strength is in its personal God. I know there has been a reaction against an ugly individualism, but let us not identify an ugly individualism with a

Christlike personality. Against this latter there is no law.

The good minister of Jesus Christ must have the qualities shown in the incarnation, he must practice the principles, the motives, and, in essence, the methods of the incarnation. This is not simply a problem of theology or of religion in general. It is a problem of our high calling in peculiar measure. It is not simply personal devotion to him, nor an orthodox attitude to him as historic and living. This thing that I am trying to say goes into the depths of our being and our ministry and relates us modern ministers to Him whose we are and whom we gladly serve, so that we can say with Paul, "Christ liveth in me." The ministry is not privileged to lord it over God's heritage. Our election is not to comfort, to position, to authority, or to ecclesiastical dignity. We are elect to that ministry which does not please itself, which comes not to be ministered unto but to minister, whose meat is to do the will of God, which is in demonstration of the spirit and of power, power to minister; which possesses and uses the personal qualities possessed and used by him.

How do we get such a personality? By living with him, until we bear not the denominational nor the university mark, but until we bear the marks of the Lord Jesus in our characters and lives. We are not unwilling to be identified with our denomination, to be told that we preach like a Presbyterian or a Methodist. We are rather proud to be picked out as Yale men, or Princeton men, or Wesleyan men, or Harvard men. But there was a small group once of whom it was said, men "took knowledge of them that they had been with Jesus." Living with him, they had come to bear his mark. It will have that effect again and it will have it everywhere. The incarnation is not exhausted by being a revelation. It is also a living personal force. It is fulfilled by being such a force. It has vital relation even beyond the redemption Jesus came to bring or the truth he came to teach. Elsewhere I have said in substance:[1] The significance of the incarnation for personality will bear an emphasis it has not often had. In him we live and in him we move. With him we live and at last like him we live. We must learn our truth from him. How else can we teach it? We must receive our life from him. How else can we impart that life? The poorest thing the minister has to impart is his own poor life. We have talked of Jesus as our model and pattern. But he is more. A pattern might only mock us. Somehow power

[1] See In the School of Christ, Chapter VI.

121

must pass over from him to us, character from him to us. Our efforts to imitate him must be more than matched by his efforts to convey his life to us. Of course this has some mystery and some mysticism in it, but let us not be afraid of either. We can stand mystery better than inadequacy.

Hold two ideas clearly as we close for to-day. Personality is more important than things, and personality means much more than one quality. "From the days of Socrates the problem of the school has been the schoolmaster." The man does count for more than the plant. The miserable philosophy of materialism and force and machinery which we apply to the universe gets naturally into our own lives. If the physical universe bulks large and the personal God bulks small, it tends to make the little universe, your universe, bulk large and the personal element bulk small. A minister showed some friends his new church, a wonderful plant, easily got by reason of much wealth being available. One of the friends was a keen, sober, somewhat disturbing man. He said, kindly but earnestly, to that proud minister: "The plant seems rather larger than the person." You will be tempted, our whole age is tempted, to lay stress upon having a maximum of things, instead of a maximum of manhood. I once heard

THE MINISTRY OF INCARNATION

Henry Ward Beecher explaining why, when they built Plymouth Church Mission, they made it so much finer than Plymouth Church, the plain old Plymouth of forty years ago. The great preacher said, with a twinkle in his eye and a smile on his face, "Old Plymouth does not need much else, it has me." Under the gentle humor there was a genuine truth. Certain men do illustrate what can be accomplished in the ministry by a maximum of personality. Why multiply illustrations? Why go beyond that one figure ever before us as we study our task? And why miss the supreme lesson that his life brings for our personal lives as well as for our world-philosophy—the supreme value of personality? Wealth can be matched with equal or larger wealth; splendor of plant can be equaled or surpassed; elaborate organization can be met and overcome in kind. The enemy of the ministry is very rich, very fertile, very enterprising and resourceful in all these ways. He dearly loves to get a ministry in an attitude of utter dependence upon might and power, for he is familiar with these forces and knows how to meet them. But the one thing he cannot imitate, nor duplicate, nor match, nor conquer is a Christlike personality. He knows that such a personality cannot be resisted, that it draws men across all barriers of race, creed, and condition, that "God gives such personality a spiritual touch which opens the hearts of men," that such a "light shines in the darkness, and the darkness never overpowers it." The place you get for your ministry is as nothing to the question as to the kind of men you will be in your ministry. A man's life, or a minister's life, does not consist in the abundance of the things he possesses but in the abundance of the life he possesses.

And, finally, personality as seen in the incarnation, and as to be repeated in us while we practice the incarnation, is not a solitary quality. It is not even ability, nor that modern idol, efficiency. The danger of submitting oneself to a masterful teacher is the danger of one-sidedness. "Jesus treated personality as a whole." Other masters base their systems upon type. Our wretched denominational types are partly due to this narrowness and foolishness. We give them a kind of divine sanction as though they were a special gift of God to us. We are fond of individuality which we interpret in terms of peculiarity, as though this were a virtue. We develop our usages along the lines of these specialties. We build denominations on an eccentricity just as we build personal character upon a trait. We successfully save the world from monotony, but that is about all.

THE MINISTRY OF INCARNATION

Now, our personal ideal, our professional model, is Jesus. We aim to have reproduced in us not only the mind that was in him, but the qualities that were united and balanced in him. Those qualities made him universal. They lifted him above racial and national narrowness and difference. Never in any age were racial and national assertions so emphatic and exaggerated, so strident and offensive as now. It almost seems as if the world had reacted into tribal days and conditions. The world's relations are intolerable. The agents of world unity are the good ministers of Jesus Christ, who live again as he lived, reveal again the life he revealed. The incarnation is not an event closed and ended. You are to be witnesses of him, his living epistles, his message, living and active, complete in him, and helping to make and show that new humanity which is renewed in the likeness of its creator.

At the beginning he said, "I must be about my Father's business." At the end he declared, "I have finished the work which thou gavest me to do." From beginning to end of his earthly life he lived as a redeeming God should live among men. The lines upward were unbroken, the lines outward and downward always perfect. Men beheld the glory of it, the glory of a person full of grace and truth. They did

once. Do they now in him and others? Will
they to-morrow in him and us? Shall men see
again the manifestation of the sons of God?
If they do, they will be glad as those to whom
light has come from on high.

LECTURE IV

THE MINISTRY OF RECONCILIATION

"We are ambassadors for Christ."

LECTURE IV

THE MINISTRY OF RECONCILIATION

An eminent English journalist was writing a
series of articles on Oxford University. While
they were appearing a correspondent wrote him
a letter with this request: "Please tell us what
Oxford is to the man who is in earnest; say to
General Booth, or any other man like him in
the earnestness of his life." The journalist, a
loyal son of Oxford, made faithful attempt to
meet this desire. It seems a fair request to
make, to make of us as we are trying to interpret our ministry, as to the journalist endeav-
oring to interpret his university. What is the
ministry to the man who is in earnest, the man
like General Booth, or Henry Martyn, or Coleridge Patteson, or any other man in earnest,
whether in the ministry or not? Maybe that
vision of a man in earnest is as good as any as a
starting point for to-day. By the path of
earnestness we shall come into the heart of
that ministry which is all the time in our
thoughts. That other Minister did not strive
nor cry, nor lift up his voice; his earnestness
was not vocal, nor perspiring nor self-conscious,

but the zeal of the Lord's house was consuming him all the days of his life. Have you ever tried to realize the feeling of Jesus as to the necessity that was laid upon him? How did he feel about his work? The sense of compulsion evidently came upon him early. Boys of twelve are not expected to say "I must" with the intense personal emphasis that Jesus used in the temple. And he never changed the emphasis and never lost that keen sense of the imperative. Earnestness was not occasional with him, it was constant. In this, as in all other matters, his life was all of one piece. Events crowd one another in his life, but events were always more than events. They were principles also. The incarnation is both an event and a principle. The atonement is both an event, an occurrence culminating in time, and a principle lasting through all time. All the while, every day, whether he was speaking or doing, his ministry was a ministry which revealed God, a ministry of redemption, a ministry of incarnation, a ministry of reconciliation. It means that at least to the man who is in earnest.

This, of course, is not a study in the objective nature of the atonement, but in the spirit of it as viewed from the human side. Much more is unsaid than said. This is only an effort to get hold of it as it belongs to men in the ministry of reconciliation. This same general word applies to the study of the incarnation and other topics.

It is an occasion for real regret that the living principle of reconciliation should have been so exclusively confined, even in our thought of Jesus, to his death on the cross. And it is occasion for like regret that the conception of atonement thus so largely limited to one thing in his life should have been so largely confined to him alone; that the permanent principle of atonement should have been regarded as exhausted in that single, perfect, outstanding fact of atonement. The work of Jesus deserves all the emphasis it has ever received, and vastly more. You may exhaust your vocabulary in the effort to state what he did for us men, and the story will not be fully told. He was what no one else had ever been or has ever been. He did what no one else ever did or could do. His life, his character, and his work well deserve to be called unique and divine, because this they surely were. But it is small orthodoxy, and not large, small faith, not large, that regards the life and work of Jesus as having closed and exhausted the principles of incarnation and reconciliation. There is a real difference between what is perfect and what is exhaustive, as he perfectly illustrates. He made things living and vital for all life by their perfect exemplification in his own life. The events centering in him and perfectly exhibited in him are not dead events. In the language of the ritual, "He suffered death upon the cross for our redemption; and made there, by his oblation of himself, once offered, a full, perfect and sufficient sacrifice, oblation and satisfaction for the sins of the whole world." Upon that supreme truth, that supreme event, our hope of forgiveness and life rests. The cross of Jesus stands there, in time, upon the low hill outside the gate. This is at once our faith and our glad assurance. But that ministry of reconciliation and atonement, perfect as it was in itself, is only made complete through the centuries in other lives and ministries of reconciliation and atonement. As one has said: "The atonement was made when the revelation of God was completed upon Calvary, for then the atoning power came fully into the world; but the realizing of the atonement in human history and personal experience is the work of Christ's divine spirit operating in our hearts." The cross is not wood that is dead, but a tree that is alive. That other Minister planted in our ministry his own eternal principle and made us to be ambassadors and ministers of reconciliation in the holy succession. For the principle of the cross is a

living principle, and the ministry of Jesus is
fulfilled in ministries like his own in their essential character and spirit. This goes pretty
deep for us, but it went pretty deep for him.
For us as for him a ministry of revelation can
only be made perfect in a ministry of reconciliation. Revealing the truth even about God will
carry us at last, as it carried him, into the crush
of reconciliation and crucifixion. Good ministers of Jesus Christ must "practice the atonement" as well as the incarnation, or fall far
short of fellowship with him in the heights and
depths of his life.

But that is a general statement, requiring to
be pressed down into finer folds. What would
be the character of a ministry of reconciliation?
In what ways can or should the atonement be
practiced? Is this a phrase for speech or does
it describe a real working principle? We have
enough popular, doctrinal catch-words without
adding this. Let us look into this as clearly as
we can. Such a ministry would identify itself
with Jesus in the spirit and experiences of his
ministry. It is easier to approve and praise his
ministry than to share it. Verbal fellowship,
doctrinal fellowship with Jesus, is more common
and more comfortable than actual fellowship
with his vicarious sufferings and experiences.
The mind of Jesus is the wonder of the ages.

Having the mind of Jesus leads men straight into self-renunciation like his own. And our fashion is to admire this spirit in him, to grow eloquent as we describe it, to give it high homiletic and apologetic value, but not to repeat or reproduce it. Identification with Jesus in the spirit and experience of his own ministry would "check the fever of self-will and reduce the swollen proportions of our lower selves, mortify our self-importance and vain dignity, and repress our petty ambitions." This spirit in him kept him from grasping at certain things and led him all the time into that sacrifice of self, that denial of self that gave character, gave what we call tragedy, gave beauty and transcendence, gave exaltation to his life all the time. For this spirit was not occasional in the life of that other Minister. It did not show itself just once in a while or wholly in one supreme act. It was the principle and practice of his whole life. He bore the cross long before Calvary came, and I think keeps on bearing it,

> "Toiling up new Calvaries ever
> With the cross that turns not back."

The whole story is shot through with it. Individual proof-texts seem almost like an impertinence, as though an atmosphere could be proved or needed to be. In the Gospels there is nothing else to breathe. When you come to

Calvary you do not experience a change of atmosphere or direction. With Jesus the ministry of reconciliation was not spasmodic, as though there could be self-denial weeks dropped occasionally into self-indulgent months and years. A simple, strong, unlettered fisherman once lost his life saving some people caught out in a storm. In language of epic dignity his wife described her husband as he lay dead before her, not knowing that she was saying anything immortal: "All his life when he had anything that other people needed he gave it to them. At last they needed his life and he just gave them that." And nothing better has ever been discovered to do with a life than to do that with it, not once, in a final throw, but all the time, as the manner of Jesus was. The proof-texts do not give meaning to his life, the life gives meaning to the texts. When they are read in the light of his whole ministry they fairly blaze with light. One hesitates to read them because they throw our ministry into the shadow in such a painful degree. We call them classic passages and treat them as though they were exhausted in their original use. And we allow them to become commonplace, even to become dead letters by this limitation of their application. They never would be commonplace, their meaning never would be obscure, if these noble old words, perfectly true of Jesus, were now walking around from ten thousand parsonages and rectories into the streets on which people live and die. Why do I hesitate to quote such words as these, "The Son of man came not to be ministered unto, but to minister, and to give his life a ransom for many"? Is it not because we have so largely emptied this and kindred passages of their deepest contents by our failure to make personal their full significance? We have made this the motto of benevolent and self-complacent unselfishness without any reference whatever to its atoning depths. We are not selfish, we are politely and amiably unselfish. We freely bestow cups of cold water in the ratio of one cup given to nine cups retained. We actually seem to think that tithing on a ten per cent basis puts us into his class. The ministry is not selfish according to our best standards. It means to be genuinely unselfish. "Altruism" is a word often used by us, used with warmth and approval. We urge and practice altruism. We glorify service up to the point of making a cult of it, but stop short of the atoning life, the life given as a ransom. We talk freely of crossbearing, we sing lustily of it, but we identify it with enduring an inconvenience, putting up with an annoyance, or suffering a deprivation. It bears directly upon comfort, but not very clearly upon evil. We read these words from Ian Maclaren with a guilty feeling, as though he had torn the mask from our faces, or the covering from our inmost thoughts: "Perhaps the simplicity of the symbol has . . . . blinded us to its strenuous meaning. Art . . . . with the instinct for moral beauty has seized the cross and idealized it. It is wrought in gold and hung on the neck of light-hearted beauty; it is stamped on the costly binding of Bibles that go to church in carriages; it stands out in bold relief on churches that are filled with easy-going people. . . . It has been taken out of Jesus's hands and smothered in flowers; it has become what he would have hated—a source of graceful ideas and agreeable emotions. In theology it has been planted in an environment of doctrine. It has been made into a doctrine; it was prepared by Jesus as a discipline."

All this is very far from a perfect identification with the spirit and experiences of that other Minister. It does not get with passion into the passion of his life; it only approves, admires, and mildly shares the devotion that was costing him his life all the time. The atonement has thus become a doctrine which few understand. For we never understand the cross until we endure it or the atonement until we practice it.

Being crucified with Christ is not a practice with which the church is too well acquainted. The cross is important in theology. The assertion of its place and importance amounts almost to a final test of one's orthodoxy. But the cross in experience, in life and practice, is immeasurably more important and more easily understood.

Shallow criticism would naturally wonder if I am suggesting that modern ministers should rush around feverishly seeking crosses and inviting crucifixions. This, of course, is far from my thought. No one cares for the men who go about hunting martyrdom, especially well advertised, self-conscious, obvious, posing martyrdom, a thing wholly unlike the soberness and dignity of Jesus's life. I am only trying to bring him and his ministers into union in the essence of his spirit and experiences. In our deepest moments we all feel the chasm between him and ourselves. We feel the loss due to this difference. We are not enough like him. We are not thinking of any fanatical or impossible resemblances or relations. We are nowhere near excess in this respect. Artificial or unreasonable experiences are farthest from my thoughts, but I cannot but believe that a vastly closer identification with Jesus is both possible and necessary to our most perfect ministry; that in the crushing ministry of reconciliation and atonement which was perfect in him we need to share much more completely than we do. And in our long history those ministers who have shared this spirit with Jesus most perfectly have most nobly glorified their ministry and his. They are not few, but they are all too few. Our levels are neither deep enough nor high enough. It is not good that a certain type of character and devotion should be characterized as singular and unusual. We save devotion from fanaticism by conforming it to the devotion of Jesus. We save our lives from shallowness by having Christ formed in us. We save them from the look of worldliness by really putting on Christ as a garment.

With all proper allowance again for his unique work and place, for the extraordinary character of his ministry, I must still believe that we ought to get into the glory of that ministry more perfectly than we ever have. With this view there are certain words about him which you cannot read with composure or spiritual complacency. Take that sentence already in our minds: "The Son of man came not to be served but to serve, and to give his life." There is something vastly more than simple unselfishness in that. This is the description of one Minister's life. Those who know him adore

him and understand him, especially if they
share this spirit. What if this were the description of many ministers' lives? Or take
those other words spoken to him and spoken of
him: "Thou art my beloved Son; in thee I am
well pleased." "This is my Son, in him I am
well pleased." More than once these words
were repeated. At the baptism, as he was
entering upon his holy calling in entire consecration, and at the transfiguration, when
Moses and Elias spoke of his death, these
sentences came out of the sky. Gethsemane
and Calvary were a long way ahead, but the
spirit of both reached back to these significant
events. Baptism is much more than a ritual,
an ecclesiastical ceremony. It was much more
to him. It is, in its nature, not ceremonial at
all, but sacramental. The form of it does not
seem to me essential; the thing itself seems full
of meaning, as the entrance upon a sacrificial
life or ministry or both. The crucifixion was not
a formal ceremony of sacrifice. Nothing was
formal in that other Minister's life. Everything stood related to his redemptive purpose,
everything was part of the eternal, divine war
against sin. He was fighting our fight against
sin all the time. His whole career was vicarious,
both in its deep principle and its particular
events. This divine recognition of this divine

140

Son at the baptism was something more than an assertion of his divinity which would be useful for doctrinal purposes. The argument for his divinity is not in these words, but in the life that justified and compelled them. "He steadfastly set his face to go to Jerusalem." He perfectly knew "the long self-sacrifice of life."

Remember now that we are not trying to frame a doctrine, but to find a personal basis for our ministry. We are not discussing the atonement as a doctrine, but trying to see clearly the features and to get the spirit of that life which was an atoning life in its deepest roots long before it reached the final experience on Calvary. In a way that is what makes it so remarkable, so thoroughly divine, so overwhelming. If atonement and reconciliation had all been crowded into one final, supreme hour, we could have more easily understood it from our own experiences. We know how to say, "Let us have it over with once for all," and how to go bravely into it once for all. But it never was over with in the life of that other One. It is not over with him now. He did not come from a life of complacency. He did not come into a life of complacency, nor comfort, nor ease. He did not go away to a life of complacency nor indifference. Intercession like his is never complacent in any world. The ministry of intercession always climaxes in that figure standing at God's right hand interceding for us, with yearnings that can find no words. You may criticize the commercial theory or the governmental theory or any other theory of the atonement if you wish, but there is no criticism of that perfect ministry of reconciliation or of any other like it. You must not by any process weaken or cloud the spirit and character of what Jesus did or take the atoning, reconciling feature out of your ministry. You can go into it with him, or without him, or you may go in partly with him. You may enthrone the half gods in your ministry if you choose, but you cannot have a ministry like his unless it is like his clear through. One supreme, fairly solitary act of self-denial or self-sacrifice will not constitute a vital likeness to his. And, as Edward Judson so finely said, "If any one of you succeeds without this spirit, it will be because some one else has had the spirit without the success." In the long run the books of God balance.

Now, it is almost an impertinence to pick out incidents as though they were isolated and special. No event in his life was bare and solitary, apart and unrelated. It is the whole both in the New Testament and in the life of Jesus that makes them perennial, and constitutes them the current word as well as an ancient word. He was the Redeemer all the time, full of grace and truth. Break into his life anywhere and you will feel that. "An old legend describes him as working out his own cross in the carpenter's shop at Nazareth." Under the legend is the profound truth that the cross was never absent from his life, the cross not as an inconvenience or a final martyrdom, but the cross as meaning that actual ministry of reconciliation and atonement that marked his life as a whole. He refused to make bread for himself when he was hungry; he made bread in quantities for others when they were hungry, not that he might feed them, but that he might save them. He refused to come down from the cross at the last as he did all the way along, because he was not concerned to save himself, but to save others. To have refused the cross at last, after having carried it all the rest of the way, would have broken the unity of his whole life. To have told a lie any day would have broken the unity of his life of truth. When he said to Pilate: "To this end was I born, for this cause came I into the world, that I should bear witness unto the truth," he was not saying something new, saying it then for the first time. All his life was like that glorious utterance. When he came to the cross he was not coming to a surprise, to something new and strange in his experience. He did not change the direction, the tone, or the spirit of his life when he started up the low hill outside the gate. This was the thrilling fulfillment of an experience he well knew and a way he had traveled until his feet were so used to it that they could have found the way in the dark. This gave focus to his work and to his speech. It always does when it gets control in a life. It sloughs off a lot of things, like selfishness, vagueness, lack of aim, and the like. It transforms a man's very language and clarifies it. Many a man's speech is like the sword that had so many jewels its owner could not swing it in his fight against the dragon. Many a man is held back by his coats. The atoning ministry will drop the speech and the stuff that hinders its sure, swift progress to its goal.

And with this life of his we are to have fellowship. One day, you remember, two of the brethren, with apparent, worldly wisdom, with real desire for recognition expressed in terms of a desire to be near the Master, made a special request of him. It sounded as if they did not want to be separated from him, as if they loved him so much that they always wanted to be at his side, one on one side, one on the other, in his glory. Of course the other ten did not like it that these two had asked for the choice places.

They had as much right to them as had James
and John. Certainly they had, and certainly
they have. And that spirit is not dead, though
Jesus did his best to set it straight. For the
business of where one shall be seated is not the
supreme thing in our lives, nor is it for us to
choose. That is not for us to determine, nor
for us to be anxious about, especially not for us
to be greedy and selfish about. We do not need
to foster in ourselves that kind of ambition, or
pride of place, even place beside him in his
glory. There will be enough of this without
any effort from us. Here are the far deeper
questions: Shall we drink with him, out of his
cup? These are the days of the campaign and
the canteen. Can we share his baptism of
blood and fire, and share his canteen in the
long march, in the trench, or the bitter fight?
This is greatness for him, for those other men,
the whole dozen of them, for us, that for redemption's sake we walk his way of service and
ministry, without thought of authority, reward,
rank, or greatness. Where we shall sit is unimportant, what we shall be and do is important
to him and to the world. Can we share his cup
and his baptism? Brothers, in the language of
the ritual, let us draw near with faith and take
this holy sacrament to our comfort and strength.
For there is no comfort or strength in any other

way than his. If it be a weary way to God, it is
an infinitely wearier way to any half-gods.

Why does the transfiguration seem so far from
the crucifixion, as though those two mountains
had no relation to each other? Why should we
be so slow to see the bearing of a rapture, an
exaltation in our religious experience? I asked
a thoughtful Christian what he thought about
when the transfiguration came to his mind.
He answered: "The glory of it, the glistening
garments, the shining faces, the visitors, and
the voice from heaven." That would be the
usual response. But in that high place and
high hour those present talked of the coming
death of that Minister with the glistening garments and the divine approval. Calvary cast
its shadow across that radiant scene. The atoning, sacrificial ministry was not out of mind at
all, even when it seemed far away. When they
came down it was to meet the boy possessed of
the demons which the disciples had been unable
to cast out. And immediately the discussion
of demoniacal possession gets going. And this
in a world where demons abound, demons that
can only be cast out by the right kind of a ministry! Our poor, human ministry that day was
helpless. It could not cast the demons out.
And our ministry got blistered because it could
not. It deserved it. It deserves it yet, when it

only stands round, rubbing its hands and keeping the discussion going while boys are ruined by demons. He did the thing needing to be done. Demons cannot stand his kind of authority. I wonder if again that voice came out of the skies: "Thou art my Son."

One other word remains. He spoke it himself. "If any man would follow me, let him deny himself, take up his cross day by day and so follow me. For whosoever desires to save his life shall lose it." I think this is perfectly fair. We forced the cross upon him. We compelled the atoning feature to come into his life. We ought to identify ourselves with him clear through. We ought to share the cross we planted in his life. We get the benefits of this life. We ought to share it. He identified himself with people gone wrong. He took their case upon himself. The old discussion as to whether Jesus would have come if man had not sinned seems perfectly idle and academic. He did come because we men had gone wrong, and we maltreated him in a hundred ways, and finally killed him. We are dealing with the world as it is. What kind of incarnation would have taken place in a world without sin is interesting but speculative. "God has other words for other worlds. But for this world the Word of God is Christ." What name he

would have borne if he had come into such a
world we cannot even guess. It would not
have been Jesus. The reason for that name
would not have existed. He did come into a
world gone wrong. He does bear the name
which is tragic in the very meaning of it. The
ministry of Jesus was a ministry of reconciliation because no other would do in this world.
Keep away from the idle discussions that befog
men and take the edge off the preaching value
and the personal meaning of that ministry. We
understand it and we easily make it plain when
in its spirit we repeat it and practice it. The
cross is no great mystery to men who really
take it up and carry it around daily. Jesus's
life is absolutely luminous to the man who
shares it in its full spirit. But even the teach-
ings, the wonderful words of Jesus, become con-
fused and impossible to the man who is not
sharing his life in its deepest meaning. He loses
the sense of values and of emphasis. Jesus himself is a mystery to the man who is not going
his way. It is not for us to vapor away, to
reduce, to dilute the meaning of his own words;
not for us to pick out the things we like and
leave the rest; not for us to detach ourselves
and our ministry from him and his ministry in
spirit and practice. He could not go half way
and then stop. He could not go up to the vision

of a cross and then back out without going the whole length. Evidently, he did not think we could. Clearly, he did not think disciples could do what was impossible to their Master. Why should they expect to, or desire to? He has his hold upon the world, not alone by the beauty of the words he spoke, but by the spirit of his life. And the ministers of Jesus Christ in every age, in every land, have strong or weak hold upon the age and the land in proportion as their ministries and lives are like or unlike his. A Christlike ministry is to be more than admired, it is to be repeated and shared. We can keep a ministry like his only by vitalizing it in ourselves.

Maybe you think there is no acute or universal need of a ministry of reconciliation to-day. Maybe you think the perfection of his ministry covers the whole case. It is so easy to take the life out of a truth by a false treatment of it. But if, now, you want to see the place of a ministry of reconciliation to-day, as you must, ask two questions: Is modern mankind reconciled to God, in harmony with him in his plans, spirit, character, and purposes, in love with him in his nature and will, or is it not? Is modern mankind in harmony and unity with itself, race with race, class with class, man with man? If the business of reconciliation is not serious, if the need of it is not genuine, if the case is conventional, a paper case or a mock trial, then, of course, a conventional, verbal, instructive, comfortable ministry will answer. But if your ministry is to be like your Master's, it must stand in your convictions as his did, as a real necessity, commanding and universal. A cross like his cannot be carried by him or anyone else unless the need for it is imperative.

How, then, stands the relation between man, the man of New England, the man of the West, the man of Europe or Asia, and the God of Jesus Christ? How do you think God thinks and feels about this man, wherever he is? Do you think God is pleased or satisfied with the man's attitude to him on the whole? How do you think this man, this vast, countless man, of all classes and conditions, thinks and feels about God? How do conditions to-day compare with conditions as they were in the days of Jesus's ministry? How did all this look to him? How does it look to him? And these questions take us straight into the heart of his ministry and every true ministry based upon his. With a kind of shout Paul's words leap out of the second Corinthian letter: "And all this is from God who has reconciled us to himself through Christ and has appointed us to serve in the ministry of reconciliation. We are to tell how

THE MINISTRY OF RECONCILIATION

God was in Christ reconciling the world to himself, . . . and that he has intrusted to us the message of this reconciliation. On Christ's behalf, therefore, we come as ambassadors, God, as it were, making entreaty through our lips: we, on Christ's behalf, beseech men to be reconciled to God" (2 Cor. 5. 18–20). Why should anyone take on himself the difficult office of an ambassador? I wonder that any ambassador in Europe in the last three years has escaped nervous prostration. Why should anyone undertake the task of bringing about a reconciliation? There is nothing much more discouraging in this world. Yet Jesus, that other Minister, undertook it. He entered into the broken, estranged, hostile relation between men and God and became a minister of reconciliation. Men then, as men now, were alienated from God, estranged from him, enemies to him because they had wronged him. They loved pleasure instead of loving God. The men of his time did not care for God any more than do the men of ours. The ox and the ass knew owner and crib just as men know on which side their bread is buttered, but the people were vastly indifferent to God. Such words as "rebel," "prodigal," "alien," "enemy," and the like describe actual conditions. This is not a problem in theology. This is purely personal, the question of personal relations, severed relations, wrong relations with all they involve. Now, let any man undertake the task of mediation and reconciliation and he will find out that it is no easy task. Peacemakers have their own trials. Let any man who has tried to bring together two persons who have become estranged to the point of bitterness say what it means. A revealing ministry, that teaches truth and duty, reveals God and grace, awakens admiration. A serving ministry, that gets into human life with help and unselfishness such as Jesus showed, calls for praise. But a reconciling ministry, that puts itself into the crush of restoring broken relations, that makes offers of pardon, and tries to persuade prodigals to go home, is enough to set angels and sinners to shouting, but it usually lands its minister on a cross. Ministries have been didactic, ritualistic, hortatory, evangelistic, practical, and much besides, but in the depths of it the ministry must be a ministry of reconciliation. It must ever say of itself, "I am crucified with Christ." This brings us into sympathy with God's mind toward sin, not as a sentiment, but as an experience.

For men are estranged from God. They do not care for him. He is not in all their thoughts. He is a part of their creed, a vague refuge in trouble, a sort of general dependence for safety, but not an object of much personal affection. Love for him is rather theological and religious than anything else. One of Matthew Arnold's friends, you remember, expressed pity for Arnold after his death, saying, "He will not like God." The flippancy was half serious. Many men do not like God. They are not in any rapturous harmony with him or his plans. Those saints to whom you will be ministers will even talk of the Lord's will as though it were both intolerable and inscrutable, and they will think they reach the highwater mark of personal piety in submission to the will of the Lord. They will even exhibit their submission as proof of their high state of grace. The will of the Lord is a thing to be submitted to or done after an extra effort, even with many people who think themselves his loving, loyal children. "The decrees of God are hard." Men do not love him with their minds or with their might. They do not like him. Except the few, choice special ones, they do not like to be with him. His purposes for men and for the world are not fairly, and not at all gladly, accepted. Compare Jesus's constant sense of harmony with God, with that of any man you know and you see the difference at once. Listen to Jesus: "I and my Father are one." Hear him again, not with a whine, not in pious resignation, but with a shout, this best of men, with the best will we ever saw, ring out: "Not my will, but thine, be done." Reckon that against any of the obediences with which you are familiar; reckon it especially against the attitude of the world as a whole, and you see what we have to do, standing in Christ's stead in the business of pleading with men to be reconciled to God. The song says it truly, whatever you may think of the hymn as a poem:

"This is the message that I bring,
  A message angels fair would sing,
  Oh, be ye reconciled, thus saith our Lord and King,
  Oh, be ye reconciled to God."

Do not misunderstand, especially do not despise the business of being an ambassador. He prevents war, he makes peace, he heals quarrels, he straightens out alienations, he reconciles men and nations. Do not be dazzled by military figures as applied to the ministry. They have their place, because life is so complex. But as between God and men, and mostly between men and men, one good reconciler is worth a thousand fighters. Blessed are the peacemakers; they shall be called the children of God. The cross is not a fighting symbol so much as an atoning and reconciling symbol. By it and on it was won the battle against those forces that would have separated God and man forever. And the cross throws itself forward into our ministry all the time. Whenever we weaken, or flinch, or grow selfish, and shrink from our ministry of reconciliation, "there," as George Tyrrell said, "is that strange Man on the cross that drives us back again and again." I have good hope of the ministry that belongs to this fellowship, that interprets its spirit and experience in the terms of this unbroken attitude of Jesus, that is crucified with him day by day, that shares the fellowship of his sufferings. Some one has said that mankind is made up of two classes—these and the rest. And this is the line that cleaves the ministry.

Still, I must not get away from the purpose of it, which is that men shall be reconciled to God. Our interest is the minister's interest. And the minister thinks of his theology as a means to an end, the end of his ministry. He is pretty far gone in foolishness when he is content simply to exhibit or present a doctrine, even a sound one, or a truth, even an important one. The subjects of his sermons are not half so vital as the objects of them. He can talk about the atonement, about the work of Jesus Christ, with perfect logic and highest eloquence, but his heart aches, or ought to ache, unless men are persuaded and reconciled to God. There ever is that strange Man, leading that strange life, full of sacrifice, full of unselfish devotion to men, crowded with kindly ministries to the poor and the suffering, ever liable to misinterpretation, as though his ministry were just a ministry of helpful service, personal and social, a ministry of good will, kindness and unselfishness. It is so easy to get that far with his or our own ministry, and so easy to stop there, in that desert of soft good will. The ministry of Jesus was not fundamentally a ministry against discomfort and misfortune, but against disobedience and evil, against spiritual wickedness, against alienation from God. The Son of man did not come simply to bring comfort or to show amiability. He came to recall men to obedience, holiness, and fellowship, and to persuade them to be reconciled to God. God did not need to be changed. He only needed to be revealed. Men needed to be changed in their spirits, in their lives, to be persuaded and reconciled to the God of Jesus Christ. Why are we so satisfied when we have simply presented a truth? Why are we so complacent when we have only made an argument? Why are we so at peace with ourselves over the exposition of a scripture or the expounding of a doctrine? Is it not largely because we have lost sight of the personal end of our ministry? How keen is the consciousness that we are ambassadors, that we stand in Christ's stead to plead

with men, to beg men to be reconciled to God?
What will it matter if they are not reconciled?
Will not both God and men get along pretty
well anyhow? What is the use of all this
urgency? Anyhow, what is the use of it, except by the Salvation Army, the rescue mission
people, the noisy evangelists, and possibly mis-
sionaries in foreign fields? It is their stock in
trade, it fits the people with whom they work.
And just as far as this sentiment and condition
obtain, just so far is the ministry remote from
Nazareth and Calvary and that other Minister
there on the horizon, for the tragedy of Christendom is not that the bum alone is alienated
from God, but that the college man also and
the college woman, the decent man and decent
woman of decent homes are in such intolerable
numbers living their lives apart from God and
all his interests, and it does not seem to be a very
serious matter to them or the men who stand in
Christ's stead as ministers of reconciliation. We
are dead in earnest about the war, about the
saloon, about a thousand things, and utterly
placid about this. I knew a man who spent the
strength of his life trying to effect a logical reconciliation between two of God's attributes, while
all around him were thousands of God's children,
not caring for God or for one another at all,
living away from him in disobedience, indiffer-

ence, and hate. I have heard, God forgive me, I have preached all too many sermons full of passion for truth as it appeared to me, full of concern for the faith, but wholly without any visible passion or concern for men and women and their reconciliation to the God of Jesus Christ or to one another. I think we have ten times as good a theology as our forefathers had, ten times as good an understanding of Jesus and his teaching, ten times as good a theory of social service and human welfare, but nothing like their ardor to bring men to God, to bring men and God together, to restore lost men to God, that made some of our forefathers imperial in their ministry. It is easy to sneer at their theological imperfections and incompetence, but more to our credit to put the zeal of their lives into our larger and better views. We have vastly more and vastly better fuel than they had, but our fire is all too safely shut up in our bones without any danger to the bones.

In one of the war stories a lad, going to the front, said in his young, eager way: "I take it like this, life's a thing that's given us for some purpose. Maybe the purpose gets clouded. I'm afraid I'm an awful duffer at saying what I mean. But we've got to work it out, do you see? Or—or the whole scheme is upset." The ministry seems to me a thing like that, given us

for some clear purpose, just as it was given to
Jesus for a clear purpose. Maybe the purpose
gets clouded, though it never did with him.
But we have got to work it out, or the whole
scheme is upset, the whole scheme of his ministry
and ours. We cannot endure to think of what
would have happened if the purpose of reconciliation had got clouded in his hands. Everything would have been upset. I wonder how he
feels when he sees the ministry of reconciliation
getting clouded in any other minister's hands
in any small town or large city. It upsets the
whole scheme if one man fails. Every man of
us must keep the divine purpose free from cloud,
and the divine scheme free from the peril of
being upset.

Modern men need to be changed in their attitude from enmity to friendship with God, from
indifference to him to harmony with him. The
sense of guilt within causes men to hate him.
Men are alienated from him in the spirit of their
minds. That old evangelistic cry which urged
men to "get right with God" may sound crude
and unrefined to oversensitive ears, but in its
deepest meaning it expresses man's deepest
need. And helping men to get right with God
is the fundamental task as it is the truest joy of
the ministry. Once there was One who was
wholly right with God. He reveals in his life

the full meaning of the words. He is the living
definition of the words. They do not seem crude
or unrefined when applied to him. Once there
was a Minister who gave himself utterly, through
his whole life, to this ministry of reconciliation,
to getting men right with God. Our earth has
seen no other such man, no other such minister.
"He that hath ears to hear, let him hear."

I cannot close this part of our subject without
some words on another phase of the ministry of
reconciliation. Men are alienated from one
another. The love of man for man is as rare
as the love of man for God. Race hatred, class
hatred, the caste system in all lands, prejudice
and bitterness between men and nations, all
these abound. Brotherhood seems farther off
than it did ten years ago. The well-nigh universal attitude to the Jew and the Negro, the
special attitude to the Japanese and Chinese,
the easy use of such terms as "Dago" and
"Greaser," "Sheeny," "Chink" and "Nigger" all
indicate the same thing. The vast war with its
wickedly exaggerated nationalism, its hate of
race for race, its false alignments and savagery,
is a world spectacle to men and angels. The
ministry of reconciliation seems to have been
forgotten, or lost or cast into the waste heap.
It used to be said that if men got right with God
they would get right with men. But it does not

seem quite wise to get right with God by effort
or process, and with men only by inference. It
does not work well. Maybe that is the kind of
Christianity that men say has broken down, the
kind that retains its faith and its hate at the
same time.

Surely, if there ever was a time for a ministry
of reconciliation in this human life, this is such
a time. Other ministries, seeing our impotence,
set themselves up, cut in behind us with new
channels and currents, but there is only one
ministry that can bring about brotherhood,
peace and good will among men, and that is the
ministry of Jesus Christ, the ministry that
stands in his stead, in his relation to both God
and men. If we are impotent here, then heaven
save the world. May I refer to two conversa-
tions, occurring far apart in my own life, as
bearing upon this matter? Many years ago I
was riding across a part of Ohio with a well-
known judge of a superior court, a devout man
and wise. We talked of many things in earth
and heaven and under the earth. I was still
young enough to be able to ask large questions,
which ability belongs to the unspoiled wisdom of
youth. Finally I put this large question to that
famous man: "What is the most important and
the most difficult thing in the world?" We both
smiled. After a moment the judge turned to

me and answered: "The question is large and staggering, but proper. I think the most important and the most difficult thing in the world is to get the spirit and principles of Jesus to prevail in the lives and relations of men." And the train rolled on as though no epiphany had come, but to that young minister the bushes we passed seemed burning bushes out of which the voice of God had come again as in the olden time. "To get the spirit and principles of Jesus to prevail in the lives and relations of men!" That would seem to be the task of the ministry of reconciliation all the time, and doing it would seem to glorify that task.

The other conversation was much later. Positions were reversed as to years. A youth in one of the universities came to me on a day when I was in residence as university preacher for the week. He came to talk of a thesis he was preparing, and this is what he said, in substance: "The theme upon which I am working is 'The Synthesis of the Nations.'" I opened a window when he said that. You cannot have a subject like that running around in a room with no chance for it to escape. He went on: "The nations of the earth and the races of men either openly hate one another, or live in armed neutrality, or in alliance based upon fear or hatred of other nations, each seeking at almost

162

any cost advantage over all others. The world
is an armed camp either in fact or in spirit. And
I do not see how God Almighty stands it. I can
hardly stand it myself. This kind of thing cannot be permanent. Somehow the nations and
the races must be made one in spirit and purpose. They cannot be united around a cannon
—cannons separate men; or a dollar—dollars di-
vide men; or a creed—creeds are not personal
enough. They can only be made one around a
person, and as far as I can see there is only one
Person. They will not unite around Moham-
med, or Confucius, or Buddha, or Napoleon, or
Cæsar, ancient or modern. They may not become one at all. The world plans may fail, but
if the world is to be made one, it can only be
made one around Jesus Christ." The bushes
outside, on the campus, glowed with their au-
tumn color, but that minister, looking, seemed
to see them again as burning bushes, out of
which the word of the Lord had come as in the
olden time.

Need I go on? Do you not see? The ministry
of reconciliation will bring nigh to God them
that are far, and there will be rings and robes
and Father's welcomes. The ministry of reconciliation will bring together those that are separated, bring them together in Him who is our
peace. The ministry has a task of world recon-

ciliation at this hour which ought to drive it to the very heart of God. The ministry is not a small thing. There is a world ministry. It is for that ministry in the Redeemer's name to perform the world task. Diplomacy cannot do it. No other force can that does not stand with the atoning, reconciling Christ. It is for that ministry which has his spirit and bears his name to make a kingdom out of chaos, a brotherhood out of confusion. And this is the high hour. It is a life worth dying for. Once in a while it breaks out in our human history. The moral ends of a vicarious life lay hold of a man and he cries, "Blot me, I pray thee, out of thy book," or "I could wish myself accursed," or "For their sakes I sanctify myself." And such a ministry ceases to be professional; its doctrines have value not because they can be preached, but because they can be worked; the atonement becomes a personal power instead of remaining a doctrinal mystery. Then this modern ministry "fills up in its own person that which is lacking in Christ's afflictions on behalf of his body, the church, that it may bring every one into God's presence, made perfect through Christ." This at least the ministry must mean to a man who is in earnest.

LECTURE V

THE MINISTRY OF RESCUE

"The Son of man is come to seek and to save that which was lost."

LECTURE V

THE MINISTRY OF RESCUE

THE methods of Jesus's ministry are not particularly luminous as to details. You cannot learn how he prepared his sermons, how he did his pastoral work, "how he managed a church or was managed by one," or any of the common details that play so large a part in the normal routine of our lives. These details are not of great importance in his life. There are, however, two questions of very large significance: one, how he came to be and continued to be the kind of Person who could have such a ministry; the other, the question of the spirit and purpose of his life as they worked out in his ministry. At the risk of wearisome repetition let me say again that my whole purpose in these studies is to base our ministry upon and relate our lives to the ministry and life of Jesus Christ. If we are to be good ministers of Jesus Christ, we must be like him in the essential character, in the spirit and purpose, in the relations and quality of our ministry. This is, for us, the real "imitation of Christ."

Now, no one can get far into the ministry of

Jesus without feeling in it the element of rescue
as an essential element. You will hear this note
striking all the time. It is in what he says and
in what he does. It surrounds and sustains his
ministry like an atmosphere. But for this there
would have been no ministry for Jesus. Rescue
is not incidental, it is fundamental in his life.
You read such words as these: "The Son of
man is come to seek and to save that which
was lost," with the sense that they state the
purpose and method of his whole life. I am
using this word "rescue" as covering all that we
mean by evangelism in all its large significance.
And by evangelism I mean all those methods
and activities by means of which he is brought
to men and men are brought to him for redemption. Many words are current in religious
speech, all bearing upon the same thing. Winning men, soul-winning, and a lot of others are
examples. They all mean substantially the same
thing, namely, bringing men to God for salvation and recovery. And while all too largely
this has become identified with a certain type of
meeting, and has all too largely passed into the
hands of a certain type of men, nevertheless the
thing itself, the real, genuine thing, lies at the
center of your ministry. A crucial test for every
man at the beginning of his ministry is this: Do
you intend to be the kind of minister who, by all

the good means possible to you, will through all your ministry daily, nightly, constantly, unwearyingly, lovingly, humbly endeavor to bring men to God? For men now in the ministry the test remains the same, only the tense being changed: Are you the kind of minister who is constantly bringing men to God? For men at the end of their ministry, the test is still the same, the tense again being changed: Have you been the kind of minister who through your life has constantly brought men to God? If you do not mean to be such a minister, if you are not such a minister, if you have not been such a minister, will you be, are you, have you been at the heart of your ministry?

I know the theories perfectly well and the easy misapplication of Paul's words about prophets, evangelists, pastors, and teachers. And I know how some men choose to lay their emphasis upon social service, others upon an orderly worship, and others upon a didactic pulpit. And all this is well if the right motive and right center be in it. But to what end, for what good are all these features of a ministry unless they bring men to God, unless they win men and hold them to Christ? Some men even affect a certain pious contempt for soul-winners, and count themselves superior beings because they are skilled in the use of the liturgy or because they are didactic in their preaching. And some men have never been out on a mountain or anywhere else in a storm hunting for lost sheep belonging to them. They hire all that done by professional sheep-hunters. And professional sheep-hunting has become a regular business commanding high wages and much attention. These men do not hunt their own sheep; they have none to hunt. And the real shepherds who do have the sheep turn over the job of seeking lost ones to the professionals. Maybe the figure is getting mixed here, but the idea is clear. The saddest thing in our ministry is this thing of turning our real business over to some one else to do, no matter what the motive.

I think I ought to say one or two other things before getting into the discussion more formally.

First: Do not identify this thing with any method of doing it. Maybe you think you could not be a revivalist or conduct a revival with any success. Maybe you think your gifts are of another sort, possibly a superior sort. Maybe you compare yourself with one or more of the famous evangelists dead or living and feel the utter impossibility of your doing things as they have done or are doing them. But in your Master's name, now, remember two things: never conclude that you cannot do this thing until you have honestly and earnestly and per-sistently tried. And maybe you can do this quite as well as you can preach, which you keep on doing, whether you do it well or not. And do not for an hour imagine that this is the only way or the chief way of persuading men to give their hearts to God. This is a dramatic way. The public is impressed by it. It is one of the good ways, but by no means the only one.

Second: Do not overestimate the value of religious argument, or the difficulty of persuading men by other measures. Men are not, as a rule, influenced so much by an argument as they are by an interest and a testimony. The man you have beaten in an argument, or the man who has beaten you is not likely to be in the mood to do what you wish. But there is no answer to the testimony, modestly borne, and a personal interest, kindly, wisely, and continuously shown. Love and a Christlike life will go a long way toward winning men.

Third: Keep at it. Make a vow now never to cease this effort while you are in this ministry. Men are always urging me to deal faithfully with young men, and this is well. But youth is not our tragedy. Mid life and old age furnish the occasion for our chief concern. Youth has enthusiasm and hope. It has not become cautious and doubtful. It feels that it must have seals to its ministry and goes out to get them. But when youth is past, a new spirit, not always a better one, comes. We preach abler sermons, make fewer mistakes, and win fewer souls. We remember the glories of an earlier ministry, but do not look for any burning bushes, or gushing rocks, or cloven tongues, or rushing mighty winds any more. And we reach the deadline by becoming dead men. But in this matter of persuading men our strength should increase from year to year. At thirty we ought to do it well; at forty we ought to be showing real signs of promise; at fifty promise should be reasonably assured; at sixty we ought to be well-nigh irresistible; from seventy on no one should be able to stand up against our Christlike power to persuade young and old. This will insure a ministry whose leaf shall not wither and whose fruitfulness shall not cease. Be concerned, therefore, not only for the days of your youth, but for those other days that surely draw near when no one has any pleasure in them.

Fourth: Do not allow yourselves to be mistaken as to the need of a ministry of rescue, an evangelistic as well as an evangelical ministry. Do not be misled by any academic theories of man's condition. You face exactly the same kind of life that Jesus faced. He knew men

and what was in them. He did not need that
any one should tell him. He estimated the men
and women of his day with a divine accuracy.
And he spoke such parables as the parables of
the lost son, the lost sheep, and the lost coin.
He spoke of the sick needing physicians. He
dealt with blind, deaf, palsied, leprosied people. He had the transactions with Nicodemus, the woman at the well, Zacchæus, the rich
ruler, the Pharisees, and a lot of others. The
cases are not all alike, but they are all like
cases that will be in every town where you will
be ministers of Jesus Christ. His view of all
these cases was infinitely serious. His words
about them always mean more rather than less
than they say. For him, and surely for us, the
serious thing in human life is its moral failure
and separation from God. For him, and like-
wise surely for us, the supreme test is found in
his relation and our relation to the sinners of
the race. Even theological competence is tested
by its evangelistic attitude. In Jesus's day
men and women by thousands, men and women
in general, had missed the mark. God was not
in their lives. They had forgotten that they
belonged to God. Those that were whole were
not numerous. You need not hold any false or
exaggerated view of human depravity. The
truth was enough to bring him from the skies.

And Jesus took, not a mild, negative attitude to sinners, not an attitude simply of pity or sympathy, of willingness to help where help was desired. You know that does not tell the story of his life at all. He did not send out a hired man to tell lost sheep that the shepherd was at home and would make them welcome if they should choose to come home. Phillips Brooks said something like this: "Christianity at last seems to me to be just a great, dear Figure standing with outstretched arms." It seems to me to be that and much more. That great, dear Figure was not content just to stand with outstretched arms either in heaven or on earth. His attitude was far more positive than that. The Shepherd on the hills in the storm is a truer picture! He did not simply advertise his services and put up a standing notice saying that all are invited or that everybody would be welcome. He did not simply tell men of a holy city with gates on every side, into which they could come if they wished. You can learn many lessons from the life of Jesus, but evangelistic complacency is not one of them, nor evangelistic hopelessness, nor evangelistic indifference. Sinners never would have come to him if he had not first come to sinners. They never would have sought him out if he had not first sought them. If you want a real experience that will stir your soul, sit down and soberly read any Gospel through, thinking only as you do it of Christ's attitude to sinful men and women. Leave to one side the questions of eschatology, the questions of reform, the questions of criticism, and just let him make his own impression on you as the seeker and winner of souls. Do not bring to this experience prepossessions which will hinder the influences that will naturally flow from it. And yet even with your prepossessions you will hardly escape the force of what you will find, the attitude of Jesus to sinners. There is nothing else like it in religious history or human life, it is so positive, so aggressive, so hopeful, so universal. If there were no other proof that he came from God, this would furnish it.

I wish this might be made so vivid and arresting that we could see his ministry and attitude toward the moral and spiritual failures of the world; his determination to recover them at any cost; the concentration of his interest upon them. It is all so positive and plain in its purpose that it really seems hard to miss. Yet we do miss it, and we do take an attitude which does not square with his, and content ourselves with a spirit that comes far short of his. We offer men another chance, we open a door and give men the privilege of entering, we regard the recovery of spiritual failures, moral wrecks

as part of our task, we devote fixed seasons to
it, we give this business what we can spare
from other business. That other Minister centered the energies of his grace upon such men.
Their failure seemed to him the sad chief thing
in their lives, their recovery the glorious chief
thing in his. They got supreme consideration
at his hands. He not only gave them an opportunity; they could hardly escape him. This
was not the overflow of his ministry. This was
its heart.

This was the thing called zeal that finally ate
him up. He had many interests, but only one
passion, the passion for humanity; much power,
but only one use for it, saving men; abundant
truth, but only one pleasure in it, that it would
set men free. And he was not afraid of contact
nor pessimistic over conditions. It seemed to
him that if he could get the right sort of contact with men, he could win them; that there
was no case too hopeless. Once in a while he
missed it, and failed, as we all do. The rich
young ruler walked out the wrong way and
left a hole in the gospel and a hurt in a Minister's heart, but the Minister did not give up
because of it. He knew humanity for what it
was and had no rose-colored views of it, but he
had no hopeless views either. The best perfectly knew the worst and had the most hope

for it. Nowhere are the beliefs of Jesus more
significant than here. And nowhere else did he
practice his beliefs more hopefully and per-
sistently. It seemed to him that the worst
would respond and could respond to the Best
if the Best would go far enough. So without
measuring distance the Best went the whole
length. He did not stop even with the second
mile.

And you cannot do your work unless you
have that other Minister's passion for men, and
share their lives as he did, and touch them with
hope like his own. Long-range evangelism will
never win a world.

As we read his story with this in mind we
shall see how he regarded and treated
individuals. We are in a sort of reaction
against individualism, a reaction both foolish
and wise: foolish because there cannot be any
religion that is not individual, wise because religion can never stop with being individual.
But, my brethren, as long as you have the example of that other Minister before your eyes
you cannot lend yourselves to any foolishness
about not caring for the individual. He did not
deal with classes as such, but with individuals
like Nicodemus; not with fish dealers as a class,
but with the sons of Zebedee; not with certain
women as a group, but with the woman of

Samaria as a person. And this, I must believe, is the divine way of evangelism in this world after all the centuries. He talked much of the Kingdom. He ever went after the people who could make a kingdom. Some later ministers talk much of the Kingdom, but make no recruits or citizens for it. Some even despise recruiting. For the purpose of Jesus, which was redemption, this method of his had to be the method. He did not allow the individual to wither. He got into the group through the individual. He had the same temptation we have to deal with men in masses. It looked then as it looks now, like statesmanship, like doing the big thing in a big way, to deal with men in masses. But Jesus saw his own vision clearly and held to his own program steadily, and the centuries call him wise. He did not make hard-and-fast barriers between things that run into one another, like rescue and social service. He told the story of the woman who in order to find her lost coin upset her whole house, but never forgot that she was after a coin that was lost. The house was cleaned, but the coin was found.

Now, take two personal cases out of his own experience, instances often described and perfectly familiar, involving people at opposite poles of social life and character—Nicodemus and the woman at the well. No severer tests

come to anyone than the way he treats people
of honor and people of shame, the respectable
and the disgraced. If the angels in heaven had
any interest in Jesus's earthly career, they must
have looked on with breathless interest and rapturous delight during these two interviews.
Here is Nicodemus, respected and respectable,
pious and cautious, attractive and decent, apparently not far from the Kingdom already.
Why not make a concession to him? Why not
conciliate him a little? Why not go even more
than half way to get a man like this? Men of
this kind are hard to get, and are worth a lot
for advertising purposes. It is much easier to
get an outcast than a Brahman. And, anyhow,
ought we not to recognize the excellence of
people like this? Why set up unreasonable and
academic standards for them? Let us deal with
such men on the basis of a sweet reasonableness.
They are personally all right. All they need is a
change of religion, not a change of heart. So
men might have reasoned.

What did happen when Jesus met that genuinely choice and desirable man? Just what
should have happened, just what should always
happen. There is neither cringing, nor compromise, nor bravado. A fool would have
yielded everything, or would have gone to the
other extreme; would have taken Nicodemus in

a rush or made a false show of courage as some have done. He might have said: "I have a chance at this self-satisfied Sanhedrist. I do not often get one of them before me. I will give it to this one in plain terms, and will lay down the law to him and all the rest of them." Once in a while you will find a preaching man, more eager to show a false courage than to state a truth in love or win a man. Such a man positively exults in the doctrines of the new birth and eternal punishment, as though these doctrines were clubs with which to hammer men, especially decent men. And both doctrines are to be held tenderly and spoken in Christ's spirit of love, love not for the doctrines alone, but chiefly for the men to whom they are spoken. Really, it would be a fine lesson in evangelism to spend a month getting into the mind of the Master, acquiring his spirit and possibly his very tones and bearing as he went on with this choice man. You may not win your man at once. Evidently, Jesus did not immediately win Nicodemus. But the case is one of the very clearest illustrations we have of how to hold your standards and win your man, of how to hold your standards for the winning of your man. You must insist upon the new birth of such men, not as a threat, but as a privilege, a requirement and opportunity that stand in the soil of God's indescribable love for the world. Turn swiftly to that other story, the story of the woman at the well, a story so easy to misread and so full of meaning in modern life, this wretched modern life with its bruised and broken womanhood in so many lands. This woman is not a high-caste, but an outcast. Judaism had no place for such a woman or plan for her redemption. She was not attractive nor noble nor large-minded. She was positive, narrow, shallow, and disputatious. She would not add much to a church. She would be a problem if she came in. It would have been easy for a religious teacher to be severe, or impatient, or hopeless, or sentimental about her; easy to think of her as belonging to a class. It is easy to forget that the class must be reached through the person, not the person through the class. Here, again, you must hold your truth to win your person, use your truth *to* win your person. Read that whole story over again, having in your minds all the stained, hopeless, half-defiant womanhood of our modern life; all the loose marriage relations, divorces and remarriages in America; all that countless womanhood of the Orient of which no one can speak in detail, the womanhood of the lands without Christ. We are thinking all the time of rescuing men and women. Do we see the

spirit and method of that other Minister as he
dealt with people like these in such fashion as
to make a model to the end of time? Do we
have his spirit for such work in our own ministry? We shall not be good ministers of Jesus
Christ unless, like him, we do have a divine
care for individuals of all sorts and conditions.
We may not make any new Gospels or Acts
worthy of being written except in this fashion.
Remember all the time what he was after. It
was not the making of a convert, but the making of a character, not saving from penalty, but
saving from sin and death, not a single transaction, but a lifelong process.

For the recovery, the evangelizing of men
Jesus used all his truth, just as he gave all his
life. He did not hold part of his truth as though
it were useful for this purpose and part of it for
other purposes. Indeed, I think I will say that
he had no interest in truth except in its relation
to life and its salvation. This made and makes
truth in his hands and ours so important. For
the saving of men he used all the truth he had.
Maybe that explains in part why he used truth
so carefully, so sacredly. It always needs that
personal end to keep it from being academic.
We always need to see that personal purpose to
keep us from being careless and reckless even in
our use of the truth. Always it is life that is

to be saved. And for this purpose all truth is to be used, for the minister of Jesus Christ must use the whole truth as it is in Jesus to rescue and redeem the whole life. Truth is not a thing simply to exhibit in the forum, display in the pulpit, or sell in the market. Truth in Christ's use of it is the thing that sets men free. The preaching man will use his truth with the evangelistic purpose and in the evangelistic spirit. And he will not fling things out, no matter where they hit or whom they hurt. The spirit of the preacher in speaking his truth is the same as the spirit of the shepherd hunting his sheep. The evangelistic purpose is absolutely necessary as the atmosphere in which to get truth, the atmosphere in which to hold it, and the atmosphere in which to preach it. For their sakes, that they may be sanctified in the truth, the preacher and the truth must be sanctified.

You will probably be amazed to discover how narrowly men have interpreted the term "saving truth," and how large an area of your own truth has no visible relation to the salvation of men, how many of the precious things you have learned have no apparent relation to this whatever. When the average minister preaches his farewell sermon on the text "I have not shunned to declare unto you all the counsel of God," he usually means that he has not avoided the disagreeable and denunciatory in his preaching, that he has spoken plainly and courageously. But the whole counsel of God is so rich, so full, so gracious, so tender, so evangelical that it ought not to be identified exclusively with the hard truths that must again and again be spoken, but never spoken in a hard spirit. The evangelistic purpose to save all life will determine for the preacher the meaning of such terms as whole counsel and others like it. "Preaching Christ" for this purpose will not be a narrow thing, using part of his truth, either the hard truth or the gentle truth in the gospel. Preaching Christ and declaring God's whole counsel will be the richest and most abundant thing in the whole range of preaching. It is more or less of a scandal that we have preached the partial truth. And we are paying the penalty for it. If we do not do better, we must face the permanent alienation and loss of countless men from Christ's ranks. We cannot touch all life unless we use all of Christ's truth. Herein is a historic tragedy. A careful student has put it thus: "A few years of enthusiasm and blessing. Then carelessness, cessation from study, no mental and spiritual growth, taking success for granted, reliance upon methods and stock phrases, and a sad collapse of power. No form of activity needs truth, rich, abundant, living truth, as evangelism does. Nowhere does intellectual laziness meet surer, swifter punishment. Many mission churches fail utterly in their attempts to reach intelligent workingmen because of the indolent reiteration of threadbare phrases and a failure to respect an audience." Evangelism like Christ's will not only use truth, it will produce truth; not only use sound doctrine, but produce sound doctrine. For the preacher this is both the source of doctrine and the test of it. His truth will arise and grow in this atmosphere.

In this matter we are concerned with all life. Using all our truth is the means, reaching all life is the end. Do not hold any shallow or partial views as to the truth you are to use. Do not hold any narrow or imperfect views as to the life you are to reach in Christ's name for salvation. You are not ministers of a fragment of the counsel of God, nor to a class of the people for whom Christ lived and died. For the sake of rescue you will use all truth, hate all sin, and seek all life. Doctor Chapman tells how one night, after Captain Sam Hadley had piloted him through the slums, he turned and said: "Brother, as long as you live preach a gospel that can reach people like these." So say we all. And when Phillips Brooks finished his noble series of noonday sermons in old

Trinity, at the head of Wall Street, he might have turned to any minister standing near with the same words: "Brother, as long as you live preach a gospel that can reach people like these." And when Henry Drummond finished at University of Glasgow, or Edinburgh, or at Yale, or at Student Conference at Northfield, he might have said to any one of us: "Brother, as long as you live preach a gospel that can reach people like these." To scholar and to bum, to respectability and to shame, to adult and to youth, to Oriental and to Occidental, to every person in every condition, in every land to the widest range of life, the minister of Jesus has a ministry of rescue from the life that now is to the new life in Jesus Christ. Do not cast away any truth that will win, nor any person who can be won. Here you stand in the tangled growth of modern life, in its bewildering paths, "where cross the crowded ways of life," to guide the steps of all men and women to the zone of safety in the Redeemer's name; to keep life from being run down, to catch up the life that has been run down, the sheep that has been torn by the wolves, the son that has got lost, and bring all of them home. Rescue or evangelism, in this high view of it, cannot be regarded as a small, cheap thing practiced by cheap men with cheap methods, cheap songs, and cheap gimcracks, touching life in ephemeral, partial fashion. This is the high water mark of work, the consummate achievement of Christian activity, that no man is by himself great enough to reach perfectly. When you can set Christ forth adequately and properly to any age, when you can bring him vitally to the life of man and society in all lands and conditions, when you can set him in saving relation to people in all classes, you may go to the head of the procession. This will be rescue work or evangelism, and nothing else will. The small mountebankery of the peddler is blistered and withered in this atmosphere. This will be preaching Christ in reality, the noblest and most difficult thing in the whole range of preaching, the severest test any preacher meets. When you can do this so as to touch Sam Hadley's bums and the captains of industry, the unlettered mountaineer and the scholar of high degree, all classes in all places, then you may thank God who has enabled you and put you into this ministry. And then you must walk with special humility before men and angels, for evangelistic pride quickly destroys evangelistic power, just as greed chokes the channels of grace.

Now, as likely as not, you are wondering what I am going to say about methods of evangelism, and hoping that easy, sure, and reliable ways of doing it are about to be presented. But, really, the question of method is not half as important as the deeper question of motive. "The evangelistic methods must not dominate the evangelistic motives," said dear Dr. James Dennis. We take our motives for granted, which is not a safe or wise thing to do. We assume that our motives are all right and that only our methods are faulty. We study other men's methods, thinking that the method is the chief thing. But the motive is vastly more important in this as in all other parts of the ministry. Wise methods abound, motives are weak or lacking. The machinery is abundant, but not automatic. Of course it is assumed that in all a minister's work his motive is pure. Surely, there is no such thing among us as a genuinely bad or a seriously mixed motive. We must not spoil our ministry by the motive behind or in it. We would not do good work, for the Master's sake, with our own advantage or advancement as a by-product. We cannot keep one eye upon that other Minister and the other on some coveted place. That would destroy our power to see. We could not stand the strain. And, surely, no minister would rejoice in or report a revival to the church papers with any idea that this would attract attention to himself. Nor will we classify our converts according to their social or financial prominence. That would spoil the whole thing. You could not do that in the presence of the Master. Our motive, then, all the time must be like his—pure enough to see clear through.

But this is only the alphabet of the subject of motive. Many motives are perfectly pure, pure as dewdrops, and about that size. Motive must be large enough to last and to move in. It takes a big motive to last a lifetime, to keep a ministry moving in power through forty or fifty years. It takes a lot of water to float a navy. The old Oregon would have cut a sorry figure in a millpond or a fountain. She required sea room. It takes a big motive to float a ministry that is doing anything. A landlocked inlet, a quiet harbor, or a peaceful bay will do for some. It all depends on the ministry. It is a tragedy to overtake your own horizon along about forty-five or fifty, or lose your motive power about that time. A Civil War veteran was speaking one day of his wounds. He had been shot twice, once with a ball that plowed through flesh and bones; once, as he playfully said, with a ball that was spent when it hit him. Many a minister is striking a town with the force of a spent ball. That probably accounts for a lot of things of which we need not speak. Particularly, now, in this matter of evangelism is the large, lasting motive needed. This sort of work is difficult, full of failures, tragic with falls and reverses. The sower of tares is very active in your field. Again and again the apparently hopeful convert turns back and walks no more with you. Men who ought to respond promptly are slow, obstinate, and discouraging. They resent your interest and regard your solicitude as an impertinence. They argue, offer trifling excuses, criticize the church members, hide behind the lame ducks in your flock, when you are trying your best to lead them to Christ. And it wears out even a good motive, unless it has endurance like the Master's. A young man was asked how many times he had proposed marriage to a certain young woman. He could not answer, the times were so many. He was then asked how long he intended to keep it up, and replied, promptly, "Until I win her or some one else does." That was a motive with endurance in it.

The evangelistic motive must have the qualities of size and endurance, must be big enough to move in and large enough to last. Has the blight of small motive fallen upon us? The small motive withers and shrivels everything it touches. Expectation dries up and enthusiasm is quenched by it. The British Weekly, not long ago, said this: "We would not for a moment speak uncharitably, but the question often

rises whether preachers have any purpose or
any desire or any dream of bringing souls to
Christ by the sermons they preach. We have
even known men to sneer at the idea that the
church was a soul-saving organization. . . .
Yet if it is not that, it is not and can never be
the Church of Jesus Christ." Test your motives by the expectation that is in them. Test
your sermons by that test and see how many
of them perish utterly. You do not expect men
to come to Jesus Christ. Very well, they will
not come. A minister was complaining to Mr.
Spurgeon about the small number of conversions in his ministry. Mr. Spurgeon said, with
an apparent seriousness, which was only apparent and not real: "You surely do not expect
conversions as the result of every sermon, do
you?" "O, certainly not," was the quick
reply of one who did not want to seem to have
unreasonable expectations. Then the great
preacher cut clear through the case by the
quiet words: "Of course if you do not expect
them, you will not have them." Only those who
look for them see them, only those who must
have them will have them. I think many men
have the desire, but not the expectation. They
have adopted a low standard of expectation.
They are quite willing to attempt great things
for God, to engage in large programs, superb

enterprises. But they do not expect great things from God. The blight of small expectation is as fatal as the blight of small motive. Many a ministry is dead, and many a congregation ready to be buried, because they no longer expect any mighty thing to happen before their eyes. Think of that story that is told of President Finney. He laid down before the Lord a long list of people for whose conversion he earnestly prayed. He had upon him the passion of desire that they should be saved. He poured out his very soul in eager asking that God would give him the longing of his heart. And he wound up his prayer with this stroke that fairly takes the breath of conventional men: "And thou knowest, O Lord, that in these matters I am not accustomed to be denied." No wonder great things happened to him. God does not disappoint men who have such expectancy of faith and have it all the time. For the vice of occasionalism in expectation is as deadly as the vice of smallness.

Many men fall victims to the disease of periodicity, the ailment of times and seasons. They look for conversions, they expect men to turn to God in January, in Lent, or when an evangelist is in town, or once in every five or ten years, or occasionally at an evening service. They remember that Nicodemus came to the

Lord by night, and conclude that is the only time of day to come, as though getting religion were like wearing a dress suit, not to be thought of until after six o'clock in the evening. They talk or at least think of the Lord as having set times to visit Zion for the redemption of people. When conversions do occur they rejoice in having struck a set time; when none occur they resign themselves piously to the belief that this is not his set time. Now, I have a lot of patience with a lot of theology with which I do not agree, but I have no patience at all with this theology. It has no reputable standing in any system. Every day with God is the day of salvation, every season is the season of his presence to save the lost. His ear is not heavy, his arm not shortened, and his heart unwilling on any day. The gates of his mercy stand open day and night, every day and every night. The Good Shepherd is forever hunting the sheep that are lost on the mountains, the Great Physician forever healing the hurt of his people. We may be complacent a good part of the time if we want to be, but let us not justify our pastoral complacency by a theology which does not represent in any measure the mind and heart of that other Minister who knew no such thing as complacency.

A whole week might be given to the study of

evangelistic methods, and we can give only a minute to it. The minister with the evangelistic motive and expectation will find the methods. No knowledge of methods will help one without the motive. Always the motive must dominate the method. Still, I must say two or three words about methods. Good methods are better than bad ones. Methods must be adapted to the ends in view. Every man must use his own and not another's. Many methods are necessary. You must use all good methods as you must use all good truth in order to reach all people. Men easily slip at this point. They try a method, hold one kind of meeting, and get no results. They therefore abandon their efforts for that year, concluding that nothing can be done. Or they try one method and succeed. Then they sit down in the joy of their success and falsely conclude that nothing more can be done. You see the foolishness of this the minute it is stated. The wise man, failing in one method, as even wise men sometimes will, will prove his wisdom by promptly changing his method, just as the skillful fisherman changes his bait and hook. The wise man succeeding in one fashion, will promptly consider what yet remains undone and rejoicing in his real though partial success will go on to complete what has been begun. The revivalist uses the methods of the revival, the pastor with the evangelistic passion will use all the methods he knows, and be at it all the year. I once asked the chairman of a National Campaign Committee if the committee expected to secure the reelection of the President who was then a candidate for reelection. He replied confidently in the affirmative. I then asked how, by what methods, they expected to do it. He replied, "By every method that will win votes." "What value do you place upon the great meetings, with spellbinders, orators, brass bands, processions, and the like?" "Very great value. We could not succeed without them." "Could you reelect the President by these methods alone?" "Not at all. There are multitudes who are never touched by these meetings. You may say that the whole population was stirred by a meeting, but it never was. We must use different methods with old voters and new voters, city voters and country voters, native voters and foreign-born voters, capitalist voters and overall or dinner-pail voters, but we must get them all. Our motive is the reelection of the President. Our methods must reach every voter within reach." And the children of light should be as wise as the children of this world. We must not lose any. This must be our passion. Captain Gracie, a sur-

vivor of the Titanic disaster, died a year after
the catastrophe. His last words were, "We
must get them all into the lifeboats." The
keen intensity of an hour lasted all his remaining days. The saving of some did not make
him indifferent to the loss of others. The
manager may get out the largest party vote
ever obtained, but he is not after large votes.
He is after all voters with a view to election.
You may have the most sweeping revival ever
held in a town, but that must not blind you to
the many who have not even been touched by
it. "We must get them all into the lifeboat"—
men, women, and children. Running a ship is
not sufficient. Carrying all the passengers in
safety through calm or storm from port to
port is the passion of a true captain. Running
a church is not enough. The ship and the
church are important only for their service as
carriers, in calm or storm.

I cannot take time to consider methods in
detail, to describe them in their working or
explain their use. The motive must forever
dominate the method, and the motive will use
all methods that are good. That, I think, is the
thing I am most anxious to say about methods,
that for the salvation of all people you will use
all your truth and all good ways.

The evangelistic center in your ministry will

keep your theology sound if you stick to your ministry. If you go off on even an evangelistic tangent your theology will go with you. The evangelistic church, made of pastor and people, all moved by Christ's spirit, not hiring their best work done by some one else, will much more certainly keep true to Christ's teaching than any other kind of church. The truth you use will be determined largely by your evangelistic purpose. The truth you discover will be profoundly affected by the evangelistic atmosphere of your ministry.

And this is true also of the spirituality of your own life and the life of your churches. You have some bitter days ahead of you. You are going to sit down in sorrow as you mourn over the spiritual state of your churches. You are going to resort to special efforts, like holding retreats and meetings for the promotion of the spiritual life. You will call in exceptionally spiritual men to instruct your people, all with a view to creating a spiritual church. It will seem to you that conversions are impossible in such a church as yours and that you must hold some of the dreariest of all meetings, the meetings for working up the church so that a soul could be reborn in it. Nothing could be much more dismal than such meetings either in themselves or their results. Wise men always know what has happened when they read in the church paper a report like this: "Special meetings were held during the month of January. The number of conversions was not large, but the church was greatly strengthened. There was a good spirit." After that the pastor is often moved to preach a series of sermons on the perils of religious excitement. My brethren, if your church has gone dead or goes dead on your hands, know this, that nothing will so surely raise a dead church to life as the spectacle of a conversion taking place before its eyes. Men do not easily remain spiritual. Spirituality is hard to keep steady. The channels of grace rather easily become dry and choked. Spirituality often becomes identified with some emotion or sensation or rapture. I know no way to obtain or preserve doctrines in soundness and wholeness, spirituality in its completeness, moral life in strength and beauty apart from a church in which many are ever being turned unto righteousness, converted from their sins, and made whole by the saving grace of the redeeming God.

But, finally, back of all motive and method must be the evangelistic man, the winner of souls. The man will do the work. There is no substitute for him. He is the final necessity. Every age is new, every community different

from every other. Always there will be old
theology and new theology, old learning and
new learning, but in any age or community
holding theology, new or old, equipped with
learning, new or old, the good minister of Jesus
Christ must forever be the kind of man who
brings men to God for their redemption. Such
a one will shine as the stars forever and ever.
The ministry knows no other joy equal to the
joy of doing this, has no other rewards equal
to the reward of doing this. You can go
through your ministry without it. You may be
useful and happy without it. You may come
to distinction and honor without it. You may
win the conspicuous places and prizes of the
ministry as these things are estimated in our
world. You may do all this or you may do all
this and also you may win men to God through
all your life. But at the end of the day, whether
the day be long or short, I know what you will
be most glad to remember. I know how you
will then be glad to go into that other Minister's presence. I know what you will wish
then to say, reverently and humbly: "These are
they whom thou gavest me, in New York, in
Bombay, or in country place. Not one of them
is lost." And you will forget the steep mountains and the stormy nights, the wild beasts,
and the battles. And that other Minister will

say, "Well done," and will put on your head a crown, and lo! there will be in it many stars. Then you will wonder anew at the grace of it all and will gratefully cast your crowns at his feet. They are for him, and not for you. It is enough for you to have them to cast before him.

LECTURE VI

THE MINISTRY OF CONSERVATION

"It is not the will of your Father which is in heaven, that one of these . . . should perish."

LECTURE VI

THE MINISTRY OF CONSERVATION

MODERN religious usage has sanctified certain secular terms, and, in part, adopted certain secular methods. Among the terms thus freely used in both secular and religious life are "conservation," "efficiency," and "by-products." If words have any sense of pride and self-importance, these words might easily become puffed up and self-conscious in view of their large use. Secular methods have also come over into our religious usage and we talk freely of preventable losses, saving by-products, and the like, as though the church had invented all these terms and methods. All this, of course, is well, though it does not seem to me well to exalt to supreme authority in church life either "business principles" or a "business administration," as though these constituted the "pattern shown in the mount," or "let down from heaven." There are churches whose pastors are perfectly good business men, which have not heard a prophetic note, or seen a vision, or dreamed a dream for years. The pastors are prodigiously efficient from the business point of view, seeing to it that all bills are paid, all pews rented, all collections taken, but the melancholy motto of many such pastors might well be, "I am neither a prophet nor the son of a prophet." Interests thrive mightily for a season, but in the long run "where there is no vision, the people perish." Table-serving may easily prevent an apostolic ministry of prayer and utterance of God's own message. Men cannot well do both tasks.

Now, we are going to consider one of these so-called secular terms to-day. Heaven help us not to secularize what is spiritual, but to spiritualize what is secular. "Conservation" is an admirable word as long as it keeps human blood running through its syllables. A preacher's language must always bleed when it is cut. His words must always be living words, like that other Minister's, who said, "The words that I speak unto you, they are spirit, and they are life."

Along with the spiritualizing of secular terms there goes an enlargement of the meaning of familiar ones. Good words constantly grow in wealth of content just as good sentences do. In my youth I learned the Apostles' Creed, and, as a youth, said often the noble words beginning, "I believe in God the Father Almighty." I still say the same words, and have said them round the world. They meant something in my youth; they meant vastly more when they were repeated in India and China and Japan with their numberless gods; they mean still more as life enlarges and grows richer in experience. The form of words remains, but the meaning of living words grows with life's own growth. "Salvation" is such a word. Once it meant saving the lost. And that was so important that it seemed enough. Anything that would set the angels singing for joy might fairly be considered good. When older men here entered this ministry, they were told that their chief business was to save the lost. Sometimes they were told that this was their only business. My own first sermon was on the text, "For the Son of man is come to seek and to save that which was lost." It was intended to set the key to such ministry as might follow. The sermon was full of visions of rescue of sinners— old sinners, hardened sinners, great sinners; and the revival was the method most in my mind, as it was the method then most in vogue. The text was a wholly good text. I could use it gladly to-day, but I could not use the sermon now. It was only partly good. Salvation of the lost is and ever was in Jesus's mind and heart. Salvation from loss was equally in the purpose of his life. Salvation of the saved was just as truly an ideal of his ministry. The term "salvation" has grown. We see as we did not always see what it meant in the other ministry which is ever our pattern and inspiration. Salvation of the lost—that is the ministry of rescue of which we have already spoken. Salvation from loss, salvation of the saved—that is the ministry of conservation. Do not set the ministries over against one another. Do not choose between them. The complete ministry will include them all and will include them all the time and in every place. Blessed is the ministry, blessed is the church whose practices and ideals grow with the growth of those living words. We are not form-savers, nor method-savers, nor institution-savers, nor even truth-savers. We are ever and everywhere life-savers, the savers of all life, life that is lost, life that is not yet lost, life that has begun to be saved. Our forms, our methods, our institutions, and our truth are all for that.

You see where this brings us, straight up to the question whether you are going to be pastoral ministers or some other kind. Are you going to take the Good Shepherd as your model, clear through the whole spirit and practice of his life? Are the sheep, all the sheep, to be your chief concern? Are you willing to-day to take the Shepherd story in Old Testament and

THE MINISTRY OF CONSERVATION

New, in the life of Jesus in particular, and let it sink and soak into you until your whole life is saturated and your ideals and purposes completely controlled by it? Forty years from now you will wish you had. To-day, in your youth, with the love of study in your hearts, with other visions before your minds, not knowing sheep very well, not interested in lambs at all, being a shepherd does not particularly appeal to you. It does not seem to have anything to do with a lot of the things you are studying and planning, or to offer any proper scope for your peculiar abilities or real outlet for the rich contents of your note books. And there is no telling where it may lead you. You may even come to be known, not as a college preacher, but as a children's preacher. Then, of course, your degradation and humiliation will be complete, especially if you have two or more degrees! But do not worry lest your great abilities should be wasted on children. Only be afraid that your false pride and stupidity may prevent your doing a mighty work among them. The preacher or teacher who can keep or set the feet of childhood in the way of life is doing the largest work being done in the world to-day. The earlier states of education are the most significant. Head masters of secondary schools are harder to find than university presidents.

Do you intend, then, God helping you, to conform your life to the pastoral pattern, to shape
your preaching and your activities to pastoral
ends? If so, we may well have good hope of
you; if not, we may well view your coming to
the ministry with modified pleasure. If you are
coming with something of the consciousness and
purpose of Jesus in this matter, we may all be
glad, he and the whole church. What was good
in him cannot be bad in us. His life in this
aspect of it was also both an event and a principle. He has projected into history, into religion, into the ministry the commanding, alluring figure of the Good Shepherd. No other
figure has appeared worthy to replace it, or
even to stand beside it. To see this figure
clearly is a thing to pray for, to be like it a
thing to live and die for. One shudders to
hear a minister of Jesus Christ spoken of as a
"prince of the church." That note does not
harmonize with the rest.

May I put in a paragraph here by way of
parenthesis? At the beginning I expressed my
satisfaction that so much had been said and so
well said upon this general subject. A particular
application of that statement lies in this: My
dear friend, the Reverend Charles E. Jefferson,
has made a study of the "Minister as a Shepherd" which is so noble, so true, and so com-

plete as to leave little to be said, but much to be done. And as a vital part of what I am now trying to say on this subject, I commend the volume and its teaching to your immediate, your serious, and your lifelong consideration.

Now, the work of conservation relates directly and especially to the care of children and the care of converts or members of the flock. Let us take the subject of children first. And let us not get entangled with the question as an academic or a theological one. We shall avail ourselves both of the psychology and the theology of child life, but our interest is the religious interest, the living interest of good ministers of Jesus Christ in the persons called children. Many a man gets a correct psychology and a correct theology of child life, all of which he declares in speech and print, at associations and in magazines, but never gets a correct relation to children. Certain churches have fairly correct theories and altogether unsatisfactory practices on this subject. There is a wide chasm between the theory and the practice of my own church in its relation to children. In that chasm uncounted thousands of children have been lost. Our theory, wrought out in the fires of fierce theological controversy, makes us proud of our fathers who put it into our church laws. One can face the world with this statement: "We hold that all children, by virtue of the unconditional benefits of the atonement, are members of the kingdom of God and therefore graciously entitled to baptism. . . . And we regard all children who have been baptized as placed in visible covenant relation to God and as preparatory members under the special care and supervision of the church." Related to this is the legislation necessary to complete it. This is our theory. We hold it firmly and apply it with perfect consistency to the children who die young enough, but our practice with reference to children who live has been the weak spot in our church life, as it has been in the life of nearly all Protestant churches. Putting a good law upon the books, even the church books, does not insure its observance either in church or state. Laws do not work automatically. It sometimes seems to me that our fathers had not the courage to stand straight up in practice to their clear convictions, after winning their doctrinal victory for the religious status and life of childhood. They did not seem to know how to hold together in practice two great living truths and principles, the truth of the conversion of adult life and the conservation of child life.

And in spite of what they said, in spite of what Jesus himself said, the adult type of religious experience and life became dominant even in the church's thought and practice toward her children. The resulting chasm between theory and practice has been and is the tragedy of Christendom. Our churches are organized as adult bodies, with incidental reference to children. "The great blunder of our churches is the blunder of 'adultism.'" Our church services and creedal statements are made for adults, people of maturity. Our sermons are for "grown-ups," with occasional "little sermons" to children. The average sermon to children, preached by a man who does not like to do it and thinks he must, may be described in the language of the honest Scotchwoman's verdict on her own photograph: "It's a sad sight." Men are afraid to get the reputation of being children's preachers. They are even careful not to seem to be getting or keeping children in large numbers in the church. They would rather have their churches known as the church of the automobiles than the church of the baby carriages. They will report their accessions after a revival or a retreat or at the end of the year, adding with evident pride the words, "Mostly adults." Adults are already somebody. They belong in Nicodemus's class. He and they have to be born again, made all over from above before they could even see the

kingdom of God. That is the kind of some-
bodies they are. Of course they may add
considerably to the social standing or the
financial strength of the church, and that is
very important. Children enrolled are in a
different class. They are not yet somebody.
They may be the children of prominent people
and worth while on that account, but it will be
a long time before they add anything to the
strength or standing of a church. Of course
that other Minister said, "Of such is the kingdom of heaven." He did not tell them what he
told Nicodemus, the adult. And a child does
add incalculably to the wealth and social standing of a church as it does to a family. Do you
remember the Essayist's story of the rich man,
the enormously rich man, whose wealth was
being spoken of in tones of awe, not to say
reverence? A plain soul, with the eyes of his
heart enlightened, punctured the whole golden
bubble by asking one question, "How many
children has he?" "None," was the answer, as
if the question were impertinent. Then said
the soul that knew, "I am sorry for him, for he
is nothing but a pauper."

I heard of a church that was characterized as
"rolling in wealth." I forget how many mil-
lionaires it had in its membership. It gives
vast sums to maintain its own services and

equally as much for the work of the world. But it is an adult church. It has no children. It would not know what to do with them. The only children it has are in the mission which the church maintains. Not a minister or a missionary has come from that church within any man's memory. O, I do not want to open any wounds or reveal any poverty that ought to be kept out of sight, but a church or a home without children is sad beyond words. It takes more than four feet on a fender to make a fireside. There must be the feet of children on the fender even in the house of God. No matter how restless the feet are or how much they disturb the fender. A table, even the table of the Lord, may be orderly and quiet, but it is not complete unless children are gathered about it.

Why have we been so swift to claim God as our Father and Jesus as our Elder Brother, and so slow to base church life on the family ideal? Why are churches so largely ecclesiastical, so "churchly" as we often say, when we want to be superior, and so little domestic? Why is the house of God our heavenly Father so unlike the house of our earthly fathers? Why, indeed, is it so much easier for a boy or girl born in the church, to run away, to get out of it, than it is for any boy or girl to run away from home? A whole town will turn out to search for a kidnaped

or runaway boy. The whole country was interested for years in a well-known case. A few
hundred or a few thousand cases of infantile
paralysis stir the nation, as they should. All
the resources of city, State, general government,
medical associations, and special foundations are
put at the service of endangered childhood. And
all the world approves these efforts at human
conservation. Now, look at the habits of the
churches and of families, even religious families,
with reference to the children God has given
them. Of course we want them to be good, but
we actually seem to be afraid to give them their
divine place in the church. They will not, cannot understand church membership or all that
it means. They do not understand those adult
creeds. We worship at the shrine of understanding and lose our children while we do it.
If it is not well to take them into church membership until they understand, is it well to keep
them out? They would better be in than out in
that dangerous period. We do not hesitate to
choose for them in other matters, like education,
but with a positive air of piety we insist upon
waiting to let them choose for themselves in
the matter of religion. We declare that of such
is the kingdom of heaven and act as though
of such were the kingdom of evil. Even baptism we regard in many cases as the mere giving

a child a name, and treat that sacred act as a
social event, calling for new clothes and the
presence of friends. Then after baptism we go
on with our adult church life and let our children drift out into the world, to be brought back
in small percentage by a special effort of rescue.
And we make much ado and give ourselves
large praise for those we recover, chloroforming
ourselves concerning those we had and have
lost. "The rebuke that comes to us is in this,
that after more than half a century the words
of Matthew Simpson are yet true: 'The church
by its neglect of childhood loses more people to
the kingdom of God than all our revivals are
able to bring back.'" Not a single one of our
churches dares to face a twenty-five-year sur-
vey, showing what has become of the children
of its members, the children of its Sunday
school, the children of its neighborhood, and
proper influence in that period. "We are facing
the most serious situation the Christian Church
has ever faced. We are losing our own young
people. We cannot make good our claim to
saving to church membership and Christian usefulness more than twenty to twenty-five out of
every hundred scholars who enter our Sunday
schools. This is a far more serious matter than
any failure to evangelize outside sinners. . . .
[In this] it has come to pass that not only the

church but the world is aware of the fact that Christian truth and Christian faith as demonstrated by their ablest exponents are not availing in the evangelization of their own." "The elementary superintendent of an Eastern city school recently said that during ten years more boys had been graduated from the primary department, of which she was superintendent, than there were members in the entire school at the end of the ten-year period." Of course certain losses are not preventable in this imperfect world, but the prevention of those that are preventable for two decades would change the face of the Protestant world. The leakages that could have been avoided and prevented are vastly in excess of the recoveries of which we properly make so much.

Of course these losses are usually gradual, one lamb at a time slipping out of our flock. And some of the lambs were not very promising anyhow; they were feeble and small, their parents not worth much for wool or anything else. If, however, we lost them all at once, as children die in an epidemic or sheep get killed when wolves or dogs or thieves get in and destroy or steal half a flock in a night, we would get excited and make a tremendous fuss about it. Unless the thing goes with a crash it does not make any deep impression on us. One person killed in a railroad accident gets hardly a line in the papers. It takes something overwhelming to startle our dulled sensibilities and stir us to action. Gradualness in this matter should not blind us to the fatality in the case. Why are men so proud of gradual, steady growth, and so complacent in the face of gradual, steady loss?

We might as well face the fact that we can never win the world to Christ, the small world of a parish or the large parish of the world, by our present method. "If we do not win from the world, it is deplorable; but if we do not hold our own, it is fatal." Maybe we have given up expecting to win the world. Maybe Christ himself did not look for or desire numerical supremacy, but only a spiritual supremacy. Maybe he and we are succeeding satisfactorily in establishing his kingdom when we are permeating the areas of life around us with a Christian influence. Maybe our complacency is justified, but it is hard to see how. On any basis, we are not now winning the big world or the little one to him. Our successes, numerical and spiritual, must not blind us to our paralyzing failures both numerical and spiritual. If this is the best the Christian Church can do, in town or world, it is not a thing to boast of. Nor is it the best the church can do. The "blight of ordinariness" must not be permitted to fall or remain upon our expectations or achievements whether in the matter of numbers or of influence. The church can do better, almost infinitely better, in the matter of influence. It can permeate life with the Holy Spirit of God to a degree not yet dreamed of even in our Christian philosophy. It can do better, vastly better, in the way of the rescue of those who have wandered away. It can do this without the help of professional rescuers if it will. But its possible achievements with the youth of town and world ought to send a thrill throughout ministry and laity. Here is our largest and most fruitful opportunity. Here we can win our largest success both in the way of numbers and in the way of influence and spiritual permeation. What are the commonplace facts in the case? The scientists have given them to us. They have prepared impressive tables and charts to make the story vivid and striking. Seven eighths of the people who pretend to be Christians in the world made their confession in youth. The number of those who enter the Christian life after reaching the age of thirty is so small that it can hardly be reckoned or illustrated. That is not the whole story, nor the sorry part of the story. Youth is also the period of loss. The shepherd who forgets the lambs he lost while rejoicing in those he has

raised is not a good shepherd. We are only now
slowly learning how to build sheepfolds so as to
prevent the loss of young sheep, or so as to feed
them with food convenient for them. We have
built our folds for adult sheep, as we think of
them when we speak of our flock. We feed the
whole flock with food convenient for those old
sheep, or food that is convenient for us. A
friend of mine owned a noble great Dane dog.
This dog would not eat baked beans. The
Negro man in charge of the house complained of
it very bitterly. He said, exactly as if he had
been a preacher speaking of his sermons: "I like
them; he ought to like them. They are good
enough for me, they are good enough for him."
Of course that would seem to end the argument.
"I like these sermons; men, women, and children ought to like them. They are good enough
for me, they are good enough for them." But
even for a great Dane dog one must be something of a dietitian. Now, let us get back to our
figure again, and recall that interview between
Jesus and Simon, an interview that should be
read on the day of your ordination. "Simon,
Son of John, do you love me, more than these?"
"Yea, Lord, thou knowest that I love thee.
That is why I am being ordained. It is easy to
love thee. I shall do it to the end. I shall
preach great sermons about thee, and tell the

story of the matchless life with joy." "Simon, feed my lambs. Look after the Junior League, the Boy Scouts, the primary department, commit the Cradle Roll to memory, feed the youth, guard them, protect them. They must be saved from the dangers of their youth, saved from weakness, saved from ignorance and inexperience; saved from their own weak wills, saved from their willfulness; saved from the thieves, the robbers, the wolves, the dogs, the diseases that destroy childhood. Simon, before I put you in charge of this flock, before you are ordained, do you solemnly consecrate yourself to the faithful care of the lambs committed to your care? It will be a long task—twenty years of patience and love and fidelity before the least one reaches manhood. It will be constant and trying, it will be obscure. Nobody will see what you are doing except the Good Shepherd himself. They will not understand all you say, or the nature of membership in the flock of Christ; they may be foolish and vexatious, they may not like to be brought up in the nurture of the Lord. But, Simon, this is the work of a shepherd, this the greatest opportunity for success, near and far. Shall I say it? I ordain and set thee apart for this task. I cannot be everywhere. This is the test of your love for me. Will you meet it?" "Of such is the kingdom of heaven." They are born into it by the grace of Christ. Never let them get away. A clergyman one day said to his daughter, aged ten: "Daughter, do you not think it is about time for you to unite with the church?" And with wonder in expression and tone she instantly replied, "When did I get out of the church?" Her father spent the rest of the day in explanation and profitable meditation and never made that blunder again.

There is no use to get mixed up with foolish questions about the matter. Children are in the Kingdom, not by virtue of their childhood or their accomplished sainthood, but by virtue of Christ's work for them, by virtue of the unconditional benefits of the atonement. They are not adults either in their understanding, their habits, or their type of religious life. They have the faults as well as the virtues of their age. They have not achieved perfection. They are becoming, not yet become. "For several years a boy in a church may be a burden rather than a carrier of burdens." He may not add much to the official counsels or many dollars to the treasury. The law of immediate returns does not apply here, but neither does the law of diminishing returns.

I am almost ashamed to be saying all this, which you may think utterly commonplace, and beneath the level of the purpose of this foundation and this place, but I remember that in this region Horace Bushnell first spoke the immortal words now known as the volume on "Christian Nurture," and in that recollection I declare again that the conservation of the whole world's youth offers the Church of Christ its fairest, possibly its only, chance to become the universal and triumphant kingdom of Christ. I am not thinking now exclusively or chiefly of the few children of a small parish, or the children of Christian parents. The children of the world, the whole world, are in my mind now. I saw an old man, a famous evangelist, lift before an audience a small African girl whom he had brought from Africa and heard him say: "There are no heathen children. They become heathen, they are not born heathen." This, then, is our opportunity for local and world redemption. The stately old words rise again and walk before us in truth and power: "We hold that all children, not ours only, but also the children of the whole world, by virtue of the unconditional benefits of atonement, are members of the kingdom of God." And with these words in our ears let us firmly purpose and highly resolve that through our whole ministry, long or short, in city or town or country, at home or abroad, we will guard this portion of the Good Shepherd's flock, give them at life's beginning the direction they should keep to life's end, protecting and guiding them through perilous years in that Good Shepherd's name and spirit, even as he has commanded us to do.

Really, the only way to retain our courage and faith about the Kingdom is to remember that every generation is new. Our progress toward establishing the Kingdom is so slow that our faith is perplexed and our vision disturbed. Many men are simply working ahead, doing their best, trying to hope, but not seeing any clear path ahead of them. But we can recreate courage, hope, and faith by remembering that every generation is new. Maybe there will come a time when we shall leap over the centuries with their slow and perplexing progress and do in one generation and for one generation the work of ages. We might, by God's grace, change the face of the world and the whole look of the Kingdom by the right kind of work with one new generation. Why should the generations as they go determine what the generations shall be? Why not give the kingdom of Christ a fair, full chance at each new generation as it comes?

The second feature of the ministry of conservation relates to the care of persons and values already in the Kingdom. Three things we have mentioned, the salvation of the lost, or the ministry of rescue; salvation from loss, or the ministry to childhood; salvation of the saved, or the ministry of cultivation. These last two both belong to the ministry of conservation. Of course we must not set these over against one another as the manner of too many is. Some ministers are strong in the work of rescue and utterly reckless in the care of souls, others weak in rescue and strong on training and upbuilding. You are not meaning to be specialists. You are intending to be general practitioners, after the fashion of an old-time family doctor. You will call in specialists when you need them; you will organize our churches so as to do all that needs to be done by a church for human life, but nothing human is going to be foreign or unknown or uninteresting to you. You are going to live in "the vein of comprehensiveness" and not under the elective system. You will emphasize the unity of life, the unity of personal life and the unity of church life, the unity of sermon and service, of great preaching and supreme pastoral care. Neither reaches its height by itself. The Irish are artists in expression. Anybody can say that "misfortunes never come singly," but it takes an artist to say that "single misfortunes never come alone," and that "solitary virtues do not thrive by themselves." The solitary virtue of preaching does not thrive apart from the virtue of human interest. Oratory of a sort may last a long time, and please many, but oratory, even religious oratory in a pulpit, is not preaching. A pulpit orator is rather a fearsome thing. You must speak the truth, you must speak it in love, in love for the truth you speak, but you must speak it in public and private chiefly in love for the persons to whom you speak it. Everything exists for the welfare of life, not for the display of power. And you must hold all your truth together. "A truth that will not make saints will not save sinners." The saved life is what we are after with all fervor and zeal.

Now, the care of the saints, especially the same set of saints, through a long period is not an easy thing. Saints are in the making, as a rule, and the process of becoming is not always free from growing pains to the saints themselves and keen anxieties to their physician and shepherd. It takes a lot of qualities to make a true shepherd. Heaven save the flock when the shepherd is a muttonhead. Sheep of all sorts and ages are rather difficult. Some are foolish and some are bumptious. Some never learn anything at all and have to be told over and over the same thing. And some are not good for much. They are too old and thin for mutton and do not produce much wool. Some are always running away, leading others with them, hunting other pastures or just drifting without intention. I must be fair with you, my brethren, and say that the steady care of a flock will try your patience, test your abilities, and often seem to exhaust the very grace of God within you. I must be perfectly fair and say also that if you can do this with patience, with skill, and with constantly growing grace of spirit, you will find yourself walking in holy companionship with that other Minister in the ministry that endures for you both. And it will be given to you as to him to come at last to the fold, bringing your sheep with you. Like a faithful physician you will grow "sick of sickness, mortally tired of mortality." Your people will wear you out, but it will be worth while to be worn out for them. Nothing else will be. Of course I am not speaking of that so-called pastoral activity which means so little and is so hateful to a real man, the mere "peddling civility around a parish," but of that "daily, nightly and eternal" care of souls, that unceasing battle with the wild beasts that destroy life. Such care will break into your hours of meditation, into the sacred forenoon when you are reading and writing; but a study whose windows are not forever open to the echoes of human footfalls and the cry of human need is no proper study for a minister of Jesus Christ. Right in the midst of your sermon preparation you will hear that one of your men, a convert who had been a drunkard, has fallen again, at the club or in a saloon, and your heart will go sick within you. This is the third time in three years or less. Is it any use? How long and how often shall you try to hold him up? Seven times? Yes, seventy times seven. You still have many times to go before you dare give it up. Then out, with faith, with love, with courage, with hope, after him, considering yourself also, restoring him in meekness and love. Virtue will go out of you before the struggle is over. Possibly it will never be over. Then when you have him in your fold again, clothed and in his right mind, go out like a knight or a crusader to wipe from the very earth those agencies that destroy men, until there shall be none to hurt or destroy in all God's holy mountain, until there shall be neither saloon nor club where men can be ruined. The loss of a patient almost sends a physician to bed. The loss of a member, big or little, strong or weak, old or young, ought to bring grief to a pastor's heart, that only the sense of absolute fidelity could heal.

I would make it formally easy to get into the church of the Good Shepherd and almost impossible to get out. The entrance gates to this fold should be on every side of it and should stand open day and night. At every service, by every means, people should be invited and persuaded to come in. And the formal barriers should be low and few. Do not fling across the entrance extreme obstacles, doctrinal or otherwise. "The only condition required of those who seek admission to these societies is a desire to flee from the wrath to come and to be saved from their sins." So said John Wesley about his first societies. But a good deal more than that is now required for admission to John Wesley's church and all others. The invitation to the holy communion is just as good or better: "Wherefore ye that do truly and earnestly repent of your sins, and are in love and charity with your neighbors, and intend to lead a new life, following the commandments of God and walking from henceforth in his holy ways, draw near with faith and take this holy sacrament to your comfort; and, devoutly kneeling, make your humble confession to Almighty God." That invitation meets both of the proper conditions, the condition of formal simplicity and the condition of spiritual challenge. The standards are rational, the challenge high and commanding. This invites men as they are to be something worth being. These notes are not artificial but vibrant with life, life on high levels. Many church buildings are now open every day, as they should be, but the doors to church membership open only once in three months or twice a year. The doors that swing in ought to be open all the time, and the doors that swing out hard to find and mostly closed when found. The most conspicuous things in many modern buildings, churches and others, are the "exits," the places to get out. It ought to be harder to get away from Christ's flock than to lose one's family relation or citizenship in the State. The spirit of pastor and membership surrounding another member ought to be so Christlike, so constant, so unwearying, that a man or woman could not escape it, even though they flee to the uttermost parts of the earth. Why is this attitude so good in God and so poor in his church? Why do so many officials have such keen interest in pruning the church records, cutting off members, and so little care to bind up bruised, twisted, and broken branches?

This conservation involves, also, the creation of conditions favorable for life. There is time only for a word on this. Only a word is needed. There are two sets of forces in every community: those that hurt and those that help; those that destroy and those that build up; those that make for death and those that make for life.

The ministry of conservation means more than simply the rescue of men and women from evil while all the forces of evil are left undisturbed to do their deadly work. The rescue of an occasional runaway slave had its attractions, but the slave was not safe until the institution was destroyed. The conversion of an occasional drunkard is good, even thrilling, but the institution that makes drunkards has no place on the earth, in the sun, or anywhere else. The forces of good must be established and fostered, the forces of evil destroyed, root and branch, until in every place it is made hard to go wrong and easy to go right. Lead us not into temptation, "but deliver us from evil."

Turn now briefly to two or three pages in that other Minister's life and ministry. Before him the disciples put that natural, ugly human question of relative greatness, thrusting into the Kingdom early what persists to this day, establishing grades and ranks in the ministry of the Nazarene. And in spite of what he said, some are called Master and some Doctor and some exercise lordship or, what is worse, make a condescending show of brotherliness. When they asked him about relative greatness in the Kingdom, he called a little child and set him in the midst of them and said: "Verily I say unto you, Except ye be converted, and become as little children, ye shall not enter into the kingdom of heaven. Whosoever therefore shall humble himself as this little child, the same is greatest in the kingdom of heaven. And whoso shall receive one such little child in my name receiveth me: but whoso shall offend one of these little ones which believe in me it were better for him that a millstone were hanged about his neck, and that he were drowned in the depth of the sea." "Even so it is not the will of your Father which is in heaven, that one of these little ones should perish" (Matt. 18. 3–6, 14). Or get near enough to hear him as the end draws near while he pours out his soul to his Father. The years stretch back to the day he was found in the temple and said he must be about his Father's business. What years they have been for him and for all other ministers. One wonders that one Person could have stood the strain of them. How was he able to say what he said, do what he did, endure what he endured? How did he live through the everlasting contact with sickness, poverty, sin, selfishness, and every other thing that drained his nerves of strength and his heart of hope? If any modern minister is inclined to pity himself, to think he is overworked, that he has a hard place and a tough time; that his lines have fallen in unpleasant places and

that more favored brethren have the goodly
pastoral heritages; that his field is unpromising,
his people unattractive and unhopeful, his rewards few and his pay small, let him compare
any three years of his ministry with the three
years of that other ministry and be humbled in
his own eyes and before God. For that other
ministry, let us always remember, was both an
event and a principle, in all that made it what
it was. Many sentences arrest you as you
overhear him in that final majestic prayer.
Nothing like all this was ever said by any
other person on any night in history. But there
in the midst of it is a single touch which sets our
hearts hammering almost intolerably. We are
thinking of the ministry of conservation, as applied to ourselves. Listen to him and imagine
his feelings as he says it, imagine your own if
you could say it, at the end of pastorate or of
life: "While I was with them I kept them in thy
name, those which thou hast given me;. and I
guarded them, and not one of them perished."
There was one exception. The impossible is the
impossible, but he had tried even that. He
would have said these words humbly and gratefully, but the next words must have come with
a sob: "Not one of them perished," may God be
thanked, "but the son of perdition." "Heaven
help me, I did my best, but he was impossible."

For him and for us this life has nothing better to offer than the winning and holding of persons in the holy Name. For him and for us life has nothing more tragic and bitter than the loss of any, even those who will not be saved.

His ministry was all of one piece. These terms we have used from day to day to characterize it are not mutually exclusive or unrelated, disconnected terms. His ministry was a perfect unity, a thing like the robe without seams. Not one of these qualities can be taken from it without tearing its very fabric. You see it in its wholeness and completeness and rejoice that such a ministry was ever known on our earth. You want to get into the secret, the open secret of such a ministry, that it may continue among men. How could he say that he had guarded and kept them all and only lost one? Go on listening while he speaks, for he is talking of his ministry in this prayer. There are no greater depths than these. This is not professional nor formal. These are not mechanical rules for success, they are the personal conditions of a ministry complete in him. Hear him then: "For their sakes I sanctify myself, that they also might be sanctified through the truth." Blessed is the flock whose shepherd keeps his pronouns straight. The Good Shepherd did it, as you see. "For their sakes, not my own," he says, "I make myself fit and I offer myself up." It is all of a piece. "I must be about my Father's business." "I consecrate myself." "I kept and guarded them." "Not one of them is lost." Shortly he will say, "I have finished the work thou gavest me to do." Need I go on? Need I explain? Here at the last, as at the first, he stands saying, "I am the Door." "I am the Good Shepherd." "I know my sheep and am known of mine. I call them all by their names." "I lay down my life for them." "I lay it down of myself." "No man taketh it from me." Will you stand with him, to-day, to-morrow and to the end?

LECTURE VII

THE MINISTRY OF COOPERATION

"We are workers together . . . . and members
one of another."

LECTURE VII

THE MINISTRY OF COOPERATION

OUR study of the ministry has led us badly astray unless it has brought us to a firm and glowing conviction of the richness and manifoldness of the ministry of Jesus Christ and of our own as based upon his. Of course this cannot be so apparent to you now as it will be as your life and experience unfold through the years. And that ministry has surely gone wrong which does not look richer and nobler to a man at sixty than it did to the same man at thirty. The deeper we get into the ministry of Jesus the fuller that ministry is seen to be. One wonders what his ministry would have become if he had had forty years of it instead of three. It was a ministry and a life of simplicity, but simplicity does not mean absence of qualities, it means for us, as for him, harmony and balance of qualities under a dominant note. Forty years from now I trust you may remember what an older brother says to-day, and know it to be true in the spiritual, intellectual, personal wealth of the life to which you have then come.

We have used a half dozen words up to now.

GOOD MINISTERS OF JESUS CHRIST

No one of these words can stand alone. They
are all necessary to characterize the kind of ministry we are thinking of. Do not choose between them, nor set them over against one
another. If all these qualities be in you and
abound, they will make you to be neither bar-
ren nor unfruitful. We take a new term to-day.
It must be vital in itself and must fit all the
others. Especially must the term "cooperation" harmonize with the other terms. It cannot possibly stand alone.

Remember that definitions do not help much,
when the thing defined is so full of life that it is
always breaking through and overflowing the
words with which we define it. We must describe rather than define. Cooperation must
mean first of all that a man's own personal
qualities work together in harmony. This does
not always happen. Men are sometimes destroyed by an inner warfare. In life's long and
supreme issues their judgment or their thinking
forever fights their feelings or their wills. They
cannot get the cooperation of their own qualities. Nothing in biography is much more tragic
than the story of those lives, often great lives,
which are destroyed or fail to come to their
highest because of this internal and ruinous
conflict. It has been said of an eminent English statesman of our own day: "There is no

story of our time so full of significance—a story
of broken purposes, of great powers diverted
from their true end, of a tyrannic will at war
with natural sympathies. It is a tale for tears."
Being at peace within does not mean being in a
state of repose, but in a state of such harmony
that one may always throw his total personality
into the total task or the immediate duty of his
life. Many men cannot, do not do it, and do
not even see the necessity of it. Cooperation is
always an external thing with them, whereas it
is primarily an internal condition and quality.
An earlier Yale lecturer put it thus wittily and
pithily: "A man to do perfectly well must be
unanimous."

Cooperation involves also harmony with the
will, with the mind, with the personality, with
the presence, and with the activities of God.
Will you understand if I say that this is not
always easy to men, even to pious men? Many
men never do learn how to place God properly
and happily in the scheme of their lives. They
worship him in their way, but do not count him
or like him, or practically have much to do with
him. They regard his will a hard will and
submission to it a kind of martyrdom and a
mark of special grace. They misinterpret his
presence as unnecessary or possibly trouble-
some and interfering. They love him with their

hearts, but not with their minds at all. If the
ministry is weak to-day, it is weak here, in its
lack of cooperation with God in his will, his
thoughts, his presence, his activities and larger
purposes in the world. We depend upon and
cooperate with wealth, numbers, and ability;
we are deferential to public opinion, careful
not to do anything our people will not stand
for, but we are weak in that dependence upon
God, that reliance upon God, that confidence
in God, and that cooperation with God that
has ever made ministries and men great, and
especially made that other Minister supreme.

Cooperation consists also in working harmoniously and appreciatively with other men.
This also is not easy. Other men are hard to
work with. They are often difficult and sometimes disagreeable. They do not think as we
think. Many of us are sure we can do our
work better alone. We would ten times rather
go off and do a thing than work with a committee. And yet, take my word for it—a word
confirmed by many sad proofs—no minister
comes to his best estate except by the way of
human cooperation. Many a brilliant, able
man has come to high place in church or state,
and come to grief in that high place through
inability to cooperate with other men. My
father was once buying a horse. The owner

was telling the animal's qualities. He said: "This horse will work single or double, on the near side or on the off side, in harness or under the saddle, in the quiet of the country or the noise of the town. He will work anywhere, anyway you try him, with any kind of a beast that will pull." The owner was an honest man and told the truth even when trying to sell a horse. Which things again are a parable. Many a man will work well single, but not in a team; will work well as chairman—in the lead —but nowhere else in the team; will work well in harness, but will become a bucking broncho under the saddle; will work well as long as things are quiet, but when confusion comes will grow nervous and irritable and kick over the traces; will work where he likes to work, but not anywhere that he may be put. Maybe I have got men and horses all mixed up in these sentences, but perhaps the meaning is clear enough. Anyhow, here is a secret: no one can pull the world's load, or save the world or a town all by himself; nor can you always determine which side of the pole you will be on, or what kind of person will be on the other side. But you ought to be able to pull wherever you are with anybody and everybody that is pulling. The ability to get along with other people, to work with other people, is one of the vital tests of a min-

ister or a foreign missionary. Nearly all foreign mission boards make a distinct question
out of this. If a candidate, of whatever other
qualities, lacks the ability to live and work
harmoniously with other workers in the same
field, that lack is regarded as a disqualification
for service on the foreign field.

Cooperation also consists in working with all
the forces that make for the new earth wherein
dwelleth righteousness. Nor is this easy. Some
of those forces are not baptized. They do not
care much for the church or the ministry. They
do not pronounce our shibboleth. There is an
immense quantity of such powers outside the
church. Work with them, work with them,
work with them. Do not fight against any
force that is fighting Christ's hard battles in
this world. The church is not the only agency
he has. To change the figure, we are not the
only sheep that belong to him.

These are features, though not the only features, of cooperation. A definition now is unnecessary. The spirit and purpose are the
things to make sure of. Remember that we do
not guarantee the existence of a thing when we
have correctly defined it.

The ministry of cooperation strikes its roots
into a half dozen living regions. First it strikes
into the region of success. Even the ministry

of Jesus Christ must concern itself with the
question of success, which is both a beautiful
and an ugly thing. If it is interpreted and
tested personally and selfishly, it is ugly. This
kind of success destroys the very foundations of
cooperation. Nothing can be done on such a
basis. The good here is so close to the bad as
to make us walk carefully. For there cannot
be any general success, any success for the
Kingdom, for the whole Church of Christ if
personal success be absent and lacking. Failing
individuals cannot make a winning Kingdom.
But if individual success be the standard, the
goal, the end, the test, "then dies the man in
us," and then fails the Kingdom in the earth.
There are two questions, one personal, the other
large and impersonal. What comes to the man,
what does he come to, what does he reach in his
ministry? And what happens to the cause, the
larger cause, the whole cause in the world?
Test your ministry, test any man's ministry,
test the ministry of Jesus by those questions
and see where the test lands you. Men in the
ministry have reached the heights of position,
reputation, and reward. They have been ministered unto through popular, prosperous years.
And it has all been individual and self-centered
and sometimes selfish. And neither the denomination nor the Kingdom has been any

stronger or more efficient in the world because
of them. They do not work with other men.
They go their own way. They regard themselves as in a class by themselves. The common burdens are carried without them, carried
often by weaker men in weaker churches. If
you are going to be that kind of minister, there
is no real place for you in the modern world,
though you may get a very prominent place.
Nor can you reach your own highest success
that way, though you may seem to succeed
above all others. The strength of a strong
man lies in his individuality and his independence, and there lies his weakness also.
The strength of society is in the strong man.
"The strength of the pack is the wolf." In
state and church, in army—everywhere the individual counts. Do not deny the truth of it.
God wants every man at his best, and the more
big men he has the more he can do, unless they
are just big men and not also big brothers.
"The strength of the pack is the wolf," but
that truth does not stand alone. Few truths
do. The strength of the state is the citizen,
the strength of the army is the soldier, the
strength of the church is the member, but also
the strength of the citizen is the state, the
strength of the soldier is the army, the strength
of the member is the church. No man living

to himself lives at his best. "Christian ethics is the science of living well with one another according to Christ." The Christian ministry is the science of serving and working nobly, never too nobly, but never alone, with one another, always in fellowship and cooperation, and always according to that other Minister and his ministry. If ever one was strong enough to go it alone, he was. If ever one taught us the lesson of fellowship and cooperation, he did.

Churches are like ministers in this respect. No single church is succeeding in a town when the Kingdom in that town is losing. Churches and ministers sometimes count their own prosperity the chief thing. They build at the expense of other churches and justify it by specious arguments that deceive no one. The thing that happens after a union revival, when the heart-burning distribution of converts begins, makes a sorry spectacle. Certain ministers are commonly known to their brethren as sheep thieves rather than shepherds. They replenish their own flocks with the plunder they get by shameful effort from other flocks. My brethren, it is too late in Christ's day for that. The ministry of cooperation will build the whole Kingdom, and if it be not doing that it is no ministry of Jesus Christ. Exaggerated individualism or exaggerated denominationalism is just as ugly as exaggerated nationalism. We have passed the days when tribal warfare and its methods look decent even in church life. Our success lies at last in our service and meaning to the whole cause of Christ.

The ministry of cooperation runs, also, straight into the question of federation and church union, about which an incredible amount of nonsense has been spoken and written. Maybe some more is about to be spoken. Men have waxed merry and sarcastic over the divisions in the Church of Christ. They have told with glee how many varieties, subvarieties, and brands of Christianity we have at home. They have been almost pathetic over the perplexity of the poor heathen in the face of all these kinds of Christianity presented to him. Men with a consuming sense of economy wherever religion is concerned pile up the financial statistics, sometimes with such sorrow in their tones that you are almost persuaded that they pay these exorbitant bills themselves. Now, grant all that without any more argument. The present divisions of Christianity are not good to look at, but the achievements of Christianity have been wrought out under God by these separated churches, and at present the fate of Christianity in the world is in the hands of the denominations which some would easily destroy. Let us not destroy the best agencies in existence until we can surely replace them with better ones.

Here are two or three simple propositions:

1. The churches that now exist could, without a particle of change in their forms of faith, cooperate with one another for Christ's sake to a degree at present unknown. We have made a good beginning in the Federal Council of the Churches of Christ in America. And we have proved the statement in a dozen ways.

2. A degree of even organic union is already possible without essential change of form or faith which would amaze the world. Only the will is lacking. God will not hold guiltless men who keep apart what ought to be together.

3. Churches are not made one simply by being put into the same organization. Marriage does not unite people, it only gives them the right to live together. Love alone unites and makes them one. Love between ministers and churches is possible, even the love that makes them one, even where no formal union occurs. Ephraim and Judah could both improve their conduct toward one another, even though each remains a separate tribe.

4. And one big church, embracing all Christendom in one organization, would promptly develop difficulties and vices of its own. We

can escape the weaknesses of division by union. Then we should need some process to correct the weaknesses incident to having only one church. The remedy is in spiritual unity, and that can be applied from either side.

5. And we shall not win the world for Christ on our present basis. We are not winning it. With all our comforting and gratifying successes we are not winning either the near or the far world for Christ. The Methodists cannot do it alone, nor can the Baptists or Presbyterians, nor any other single church. A divided Protestantism cannot do it. Maybe even a Protestantism united could not do it alone. Romanism cannot do it. We could not all do it if we were only formally united. Maybe if we all had the spirit of Christ toward the world and toward one another, whether in one body or many, we should soon see the earth filled with the knowledge of the glory of the Lord. If we were really one, as Christ prayed we might be, not one big ecclesiasticism for which he never prayed, we should be well-nigh irresistible. He and his Father were one, not as an ecclesiasticism with all its perils, but one in their common purpose, one in their mutual regard, one in their deep and holy love, one in their redeeming attitude to the world. It is not to-day, it never was, the formal union of the churches, that is lacking

to make the church one as Jesus and the Father were one, or lacking to make the churches supremely efficient. It is the lack of the common purpose, the mutual regard, the deep and holy love for one another and the world, the redemptive attitude that must ever mark the church and its ministry. The incarnation, the atonement, the cross must be in the life of all the churches, not as the doctrines they preach, but as the principles by which they live and live together. Thus, and thus only, shall we get rid of our airs, our pretensions, our partisanships, and our weaknesses. Who are we, any of us, that by reason of age or history, of size or strength, of wealth or standing, we should put on airs and assume special standing in Christ's kingdom? that we should repudiate and discredit those whom God has honored and manifestly approved? Who are we that we should go about saying "I am of Paul," or "I am of Apollos," or "I am of Peter," or, with special assumption, "I am of Christ"? Is not this the way men of the world speak?

"What, then, is Apollos? And what is Paul? They are just God's servants, through whose efforts, and as the Lord granted power to each, you accepted the faith. I planted and Apollos watered; but it was God who was, all the time, giving the increase. So that neither the planter nor the waterer is of any importance. God who gives the increase is all in all. Now in aim and purpose the planter and the waterer are one; and yet each will receive his own special reward, answering to his own special work. Apollos and I are simply fellow workers for and with God, and you are God's field—God's building."

Any kind of spiritual pride or self-conceit is hateful and ugly—ugly like national pride and contempt for small states. Some of the best churches in this world are small. The saving remnant is not usually a majority. Ecclesiastical pride, assumption of self-conceit is about the worst kind there is. This ugly thing can be cured only by an overwhelming loyalty to Christ which will look at all his flock through his eyes.

6. We shall not unite Protestantism, nor Christendom, nor any divided portions thereof, to any purpose by any mechanical process or on any small basis. We may agree on a form of government, or a doctrinal statement, or about the ministry and the sacraments, and may thus make a formal union. We may even unite on the grounds of economy to stop the waste of men and money. There is a desire for union that is based solely upon the wish to avoid waste and conflict, not upon the deep desire

for harmony and spiritual efficiency. The motive is not big enough to carry the movement. No union will answer Christ's prayer or the needs of the world except a vital, living union, manifesting itself in a threefold passion: 1. A common, passionate opposition to the evil in the world. 2. A common, passionate consecration to the redemption and welfare of the world. 3. A common, passionate devotion and obedience to Jesus Christ the Redeemer and Lord of the world.

The evil of the world is a fierce, monstrous thing. The destruction of human character by this evil is overwhelming. Never say one good word for evil, never cease your warfare against it in all its hideous forms. Rejoice in and work with any ally who will help destroy it. You remember the story there in that old record. The disciples said to that other Minister: "Master, we saw one casting out devils in thy name, and we forbad him because he was not a member of our company." Early, you see, that spirit got into the church. It abides to this day. I will not add to our unhappy relations by quoting sentences in the same spirit uttered in far more recent times. Let those who have this spirit have it and bear the responsibility for it, whether they keep silence or flaunt their view in the face of Christendom. I commend this instead, the utterance of One whose heart the evil of the world broke and keeps broken: "Forbid him not: for he that is not against us is for us." When there are devils to be cast out we must all lay to with any club that comes handy and work with any ally who will honestly and effectively help. Casting out devils is not a nice business. You may have to use and cooperate with a lot of unordained and even unbaptized men in the process. If you have the passionate opposition to evil which the Master had, you will gladly unite with all the foes of evil to rid the world of it.

Why is it so hard even in the Christian Church to maintain a constant, passionate consecration to human welfare and redemption? We readily go into an occasional fight with heartiness and energy. We have spasms of consecration to phases of human welfare, but no steadiness, no lifelong passion, no zeal that eats us up year in and year out. Our battles are short, our furloughs long and out of proportion. Just now we are about to have a spasm of such constructive devotion to repair the ravages of the world war. But it needs a crisis, it has always needed a crisis to drive us back into the heart of God and to awaken in us even a spasm of the kind of consecration needed for world redemption. Of course this world war puts such a burden in a striking way upon us, just as other crises have done. The war brings in its train a perfectly huge moral and social ruin. We are eager to do our best in the face of it. "God seems to be turning another corner in human history, and we are willing to help him do it." But turning corners in history, coming once in a while to the help of the Lord against the mighty, meeting crises in world life, are not the chief things nor the best way, though it has often seemed so. The dramatic and urgent makes excessive appeal to us. What corners and crises would have been avoided in human history if from the days of Jesus to this day his church had been one, and one with him in a positive, constant, passionate consecration to the welfare and redemption of mankind. I make no plea that we shall have a zeal to get together as though that were an end in itself. Getting together is often utterly shallow and fruitless, a process without any moral passion in it. A zeal to get together is a very different thing from a holy zeal to get the world forward toward the new heavens and the new earth. Such consecration is too rare. Its possessors are regarded as singular and inclined to be religious overmuch. We have all these emotions under quite too perfect control. Only on occasion do we let them have free course. The churches in any town are marked by the calmness, the self-restraint, the ordinariness of their consecration, the humdrum of their life, the lack of daring and heroism in their adventure, and the occasionalness and conservatism of their positive devotion. Now, how can there be a ministry of cooperation or any approach to union in an atmosphere like that?

Meantime one crisis follows another and the divided church tries frantically to meet these crises as they arise, failing to do it and failing to see that a church united in spirit and passionately consecrated to the welfare and redemption of the world could have prevented, could now prevent many of the cataclysms and storms, the wrecks and ruin, the devastations and destructions which it vainly seeks to repair and heal. Is it always to go on this way? In the little world and the big one is Christianity to be helpless by reason of its pettiness and complacency, or shall we follow the more excellent way which God has shown us? If there is no way but by revolution and crash, then let us have that way, and make the best of it, but let us not glorify crisis and excuse our lack of consecration as though it were a good way.

Are the churches in any town one in a common, passionate devotion to Jesus Christ, the

THE MINISTRY OF COOPERATION

Redeemer and Lord of the world? They are quick to affirm his lordship as a doctrinal test which sets the orthodox sheep in one group and puts the unorthodox goats where they belong, but a doctrinal affirmation may be very firmly and noisily made in a body whose personal devotion is very weak and vague. Admiration of Jesus is widespread, the praise of his character, his words, his deeds is in all the churches. We speak tenderly of him and sing rapturously of him, but even the members of a given local church are not conscious of being one with one another in a common, passionate devotion to him, their Redeemer from sin and the Lord of their lives. Much less are the churches in a town so united. One does not like to speak of the vast and paralyzing unconsciousness of Jesus the Redeemer and Lord of life which pervades the churches that bear his name, the unconsciousness of him which permits people to go on day by day as if he were not.

Maybe this is the best we can do. Maybe we can expect nothing else. Maybe this is good enough. Maybe we can look for no better cooperation than we now have. Maybe the basis of cooperation has not yet appeared. I do not believe it. We go slowly, all too slowly, toward it, but some day the followers of Christ must surely be one in the threefold passion:

1. A common, passionate opposition to the evil in the world. 2. A common, passionate consecration to the redemption and welfare of the world. 3. A common, passionate devotion and obedience to Jesus Christ the Redeemer and Lord of the world. This would unite us in the passion of supreme aims and high purposes, and would be a token of strength. Anything else would get us together on a basis of low moral energy and would be a sign of weakness. It is for us to bring this passion into our near, small world without waiting for it to come in the far, big world. For thus it will come in the earth as it has already come in the heavens.

The ministry of cooperation has its roots also in the soil of Christian tolerance, tolerance both in small and in large relations. One hesitates to use that noble word because of the ignoble meanings that have come to be associated with it. For when tolerance is identified with indifferentism, and the "mush of concession," then intolerance, hot and fierce, seems to be virtue. Better ten thousand times an unyielding intolerance than such a spirit as that. Nor is toleration any better. This only mixes an element of condescension and patronage with the attitude of indifference. And neither is to be endured. There is a false tolerance which is very popular with some who wish to be thought broad and liberal. This is the tolerance which sees no differences in things that differ, which declares that one view is as good as another, and that it does not matter what a man believes or where he belongs. This is the spirit that approves all churches and is worth nothing to any. It agrees with everybody and goes about in an eternal attitude of bland and tiresome amiability which it mistakes for tolerance. The doctrinal cloud is weasel, camel, or whale, either or all.

What, then, is tolerance and what are its applications in any true minister's life? It surely is not a habit one may put on nor a formal attitude one may assume, but a spirit filling one's deepest convictions and firmest opinions, and determining one's personal relations with other men. It is not a quality that belongs to a weak or flabby mind, a vague faith or a feeble personality. It is not founded upon lack of conviction or upon uncertainty, but upon depth of conviction and wealth of certainty. It can be found only in the man who is the captain of his own soul in all that soul's positive relation to truth, to experience, and to human life. If positiveness be lacking, no tolerance is possible; if positiveness goes wrong, it becomes bigotry. If, on the other hand, positiveness be filled with respect for other personalities, charity toward other views, though it does not hold them, spiritual sympathy and insight which recognizes that truth is larger than any one man's hold upon it and life larger than any one man's possession of it, then tolerance is born, born of positiveness and breadth, assurance and sympathy.

I am always thinking of that other Minister who was the living definition of everything that was best. If anyone ever had the right to be intolerant he had that right. He knew the truth as no one else knew it. He possessed wisdom as no one else possessed it. In the realm of life and the things of the spirit he walked the way of infallibility as no one else ever did. In character and conduct he was blameless and perfect as no one of his contemporaries was. If ever the intolerant attitude and spirit could be justified in anyone, they could be justified in him. He had to deal with men who were narrow, shallow, mistaken, and stubborn. He knew what was in the men around him. The disciples were as difficult to work with as any official board, vestry, or session that any modern minister has to deal with. In our modern life the narrowness is not all outside of the pulpit. You may cause as many trials as you will suffer. But our Master saw underneath all the ignorance and narrowness the essential integrity of every other soul, the possible growth and outcome in every man, and never spoiled another soul or his own by any intolerant assertion of his own superiority. He did not weakly yield nor weakly bluster and assert his prerogatives. He simply planted his own perfect life in perfect tolerance in the lives of those other men and transformed them into the same image. The process was slow and the result imperfect, but the method was perfect for him and for us, except that always we must be even more modest than he was, always less sure of the absolute correctness of our opinions and our lives. If you want, then, to see tolerance alive, study that other Minister in whom it perfectly dwelt.

You will have abundant opportunity and necessity for the exercise and practice of this spirit in your ministry of cooperation, just as your brethren will. Just in so far as your own faith is positive, your own vision large, your own life full, you will be sorely tried by contact with those whose faith is feeble, vision narrow, and life meager. They will be in your official boards or vestries or sessions. They will seek to determine the policy of your church and the ideals of your ministry. They will measure your preaching by their standards and will balk your largest, most spiritual, most cherished

plans. They will set their own utter intolerance
over against you until you will feel that no cooperation is possible between you and them. I
dread for you the trying, difficult day that will
come early in your ministry when this assault
comes upon you. It will come partly because
you are young and inexperienced. You will be
liable to make mistakes, and bring it on. Many
a minister has had his spirit broken under it,
and has either left the ministry to escape the
intolerance of other men or has himself become
hard and intolerant, meeting intolerance with
intolerance, giving like for like, and finally destroying his own best spirit. From within your
own church, from your own brethren, laymen
and ministers, from other churches in the town
and the world, from within your own soul,
from the world itself this grinding, crushing
force will come upon you, assailing you where
you are most sensitive and susceptible to hurt.
It will wear out your soul if you allow it to do so,
as it tried to wear out the soul of your Master.
Now, when it comes and as it comes, remember
that you can have a ministry of tolerance and
cooperation, or you can have a ministry of intolerance without cooperation, but you cannot
have both. Remember that the life of your
own spirit is involved, and never even for an
hour meet littleness with littleness, hardness

with hardness. The process will be slow, but the life that is large, the faith that is vital, the humanity that is Christlike even toward intolerant men will win, will win in your own life and at last in the lives of those other men. Neither you nor your ministry can get on in the world without this spirit. You can live in the atmosphere of loyalty and love, but no ministry of Jesus can live in the atmosphere of bigotry.

The ministry of cooperation has both root and fruit in a true Christian leadership, another word one hesitates to use. If words grow weary when overworked, this one must long since have reached the state of complete exhaustion. A speech is hardly complete unless it bewails the lack of leadership and asserts the need of it. When Lord Salisbury asked Lord Roberts to go to South Africa, he said, "We are finding that this war depends upon the generals." This sentence is much quoted and remembered to this day, particularly by those who are modestly conscious of being generals and having the capacity for large leadership. And the general, the military commander, promptly becomes the ideal, the type of leader which gets into our minds. And we do not see how even a brief discussion of leadership gets into a study of the ministry of cooperation.

These, surely, are terms almost mutually exclusive. But this is exactly the place for this word. These are correlated, mutually inclusive terms. Neither can exist without the other. There can be no leadership without cooperation. One who cannot secure cooperation may be very able and advanced, independent and solitary, but he is not a leader. One may cooperate without advancing, cooperate on low levels, cooperate without goals or progress toward them, without being a leader. But a ministry cannot be at its best unless it is a ministry which is both getting forward and leading forward. It is not a true ministry, a ministry of the best sort, when it is simply going forward, no matter how bravely and independently. For these are overwhelmingly personal terms, that cannot really be thought of apart from close personal relations. Neither dwells chiefly in the realm of ideas. They live and move and have their being in the realm of personal life. The life in the leader is the light of men. It is not independent or abstract.

Of course a leader must be in advance, must have a goal, must know where that goal is and the way to it, but, of course also, he is not a leader if the goal is simply his individual goal which he is seeking to reach by himself, not caring what becomes of the others. Lowell said of Garrison: "He is so used to standing alone that, like Daniel Boone, he moves away as the world creeps up to him and goes further into the wilderness. He considers every step a step forward, even though it be over the edge of a precipice." But that is not real leadership. Remember what Matthew Arnold said of his father:

> "Thou, thou wouldst not be saved alone.
>
> .   .   .   .   .
>
> Therefore to thee it was given
> Many to bring with thyself."

You are expecting to be leaders in the realm of the life of the spirit. You ought to be. There is tragic need of leadership in this realm. Your ideal is not the commander, though even he can do nothing without perfect cooperation, but the Shepherd! That noble figure breaks into our ministry at every turn, breaks in just at those points where we least look for it, breaks in with those qualities that make us bow our heads and hold our hearts with wonder. Just when we are tempted to be self-assertive and masterful in our leadership, or "magerful," as Sentimental Tommy put it, we get the vision of that other One and hear the words, "He walks at the head of them and the sheep follow him." The wisdom of the leader is superior. In the realm of religion you ought to be the wisest person in your church. The vision of the leader should be clear, the clearest in the parish. He, better than any one else, should know the whither, the goal, and the way. The heart of the leader should be the bravest, so that he should never lose heart for himself or his flock. His heart should also be the most patient and tender, that he should not lose any of them while he impatiently and zealously presses on toward that desired haven. You may well be the ablest person in your group. You will need all the ability you have; but if you use it proudly, with contempt or scorn for those less able, then you fall far short of the ability that makes a leader.

For your cooperation as a leader is not alone with other leaders, able men like yourselves. It is with your flock, with those to whom you always modestly and humbly refer as your followers. Modestly and humbly, I have said, and let the words stand. For that God should put us into this ministry in a place of leadership, the leadership of human life for Christ's sake, ought to destroy all self-conceit and spiritual pride in us, and make us to walk humbly as we remember our real Leader, evermore saying of ourselves, "I am not worthy to unlatch his shoes," while we go on straightening paths that are crooked, and making smooth the places that are rough, making them straight and smooth for human feet. And some of those we lead are old, and some are lame, and some are only learning to walk, and no one of them ever went this way before. The leadership of Jesus is our inspiration and our model in this ministry of cooperation, and we have no other. Secondary models will not answer.

And now, as our frequent manner is, I flee from these more particular statements to a verbal city of refuge and declare in a large and ample way that the ministry of cooperation roots at last in a man's spirit. This is made up, indeed, of many qualities, but it is something other and more or less than their sum. Some qualities count for far more than others, even though all are valuable. But a man's spirit is not identical with his particular qualities and characteristics. Our fathers used to classify men according to their disposition. Some were men of good disposition, others of bad, and the worst thing to be said of a man was that he had a mean disposition. No matter what else he had, this was a fatal characterization. The men of good will, the men of good disposition, the men of right spirit do at last hold the world in their hands for its salvation. An ugly spirit may win temporary victories for itself, but it can win no victories at all for the kingdom of good will. The churches are greatly concerned about the men who are coming into the ministry, concerned about their ability, wondering whether they are equal to the men going into other callings; concerned about their motives, wondering what brings them into the ministry; concerned about their characters, wondering whether they are really men of God, with clean hands and pure hearts; but the churches have no deeper concern than for the spirit of the men coming to be their leaders. Are they men of good will? Is their ability sustained by a spirit that will make their ability effective? Have they that human spirit that counts for so much, that spirit the lack of which hinders even the grace of God in its working? Will these coming ministers, vastly better than past or present ministers have done, recognize and unite with all the cooperative forces that work for the life of man, and all the cooperative persons who are casting out demons and building society in strength and beauty? Will they be the kind of men who will say with a historic religious leader: "Is thy heart herein as my heart? If it be give me thy hand"? That is to say, do you love the things that I love, are you devoted to the cause to which I am devoted, do you hate the things that I hate, do you follow the Master that I follow? If so, let us join hands, not simply shake hands as a sign of good will, but let us unite in the fellowship of worship and of service.

It does not take a very large fly to spoil the ointment of this spirit, or a very large fox to cut its vine so that it will bear no fruit. A little self-conceit or denominational conceit will do it. A lack of genuine humility will do it. Jealousy, personal or denominational, will eat the life out of it. Every year I bring many times to myself and my brethren the story of that wonderful man John the Baptist, and pray that a double portion of his spirit may fall upon us. It is so easy to have part of his spirit, so easy for one man to recognize the ability of another one, so easy for one preacher to praise the greatness of another. It is a mark of one's own greatness that he can recognize and admit the greatness of other men in his own field. But it is a deeper test of one's spirit to recognize and admit that other men are greater than himself in his own field, and to do it with personal joy. John was not old and through with it all, he was young and facing it all, when his heart leaped up to recognize that One greater than himself had come. It is good to look through a soul like that, without any mock humility in it, with no fear of Herod or generosity to the vipers, but with the truest humility ever seen on our planet, in its recognition of another, a neighbor, of his own age, and a prophet. Can you bear that test, do you think? Are you going to be happy or unhappy when the essence of that situation is repeated in your own life and experience? If you can meet that test with others like it, you may enter this ministry of cooperation with a high heart, and this ministry may receive you with drums beating and colors flying. After all, the spirit of your ministry will depend upon the spirit of the minister.

Finally, this ministry of cooperation will work in the whole world. Nationalism is good unless it be exaggerated, self-assertive, swollen with pride. Then it becomes an enemy to civilization and a curse to the world, for "above all nations is humanity," the humanity that dwells in large state and small one alike, the humanity of black race, yellow race, and white race alike. The doctrine of human brotherhood is in a very perplexing position in view of the war. Our feeble assertion and wretched practice of the truth of brotherhood is one of the fruitful causes of the war. The caste system in our practice between races and classes has helped to make our testimony feeble and ineffective at a point where it should have been strong. Denominationalism is good unless it be exaggerated, intolerant, vain, swollen with spiritual pride in its history or wealth, size, or achievements. Then it becomes a menace to Christianity itself, a blight upon religion instead of a blessing in the name of religion, for above all denominations is Christianity, the Christianity that dwells alike in large denominations and small, the Christianity for all the races, the Christianity which is the master but not the servant of the denominations. Individualism is good unless it be exaggerated, conceited, aloof and exclusive, dwelling apart, intolerant and bigoted. Then it breaks the brotherhood that is in Christ, sets up false standards in the church, and holds Christianity back in town and world.

Against all these things set your faces and your hearts. Neither Germany, nor England, nor America is to be over all, the ruler of the world. Neither Anglo-Saxon, Teuton, Slav, nor Oriental is to sit on every throne and control the lands and seas that belong to mankind. Neither episcopacy nor independence, Romanism nor Protestantism is to have lordship in the Church of Christ. Nor are we men to be called Master, Master. There is to be but one King over all, one church of the living God, one Master of men, even Christ.

The kingdom of God in the whole earth is the final unit. The will of God is the final rule and authority in the earth. For that through the ages we have prayed. For that let us labor and pray. For that let us work together, together with one another and with God.

LECTURE VIII
THE MINISTRY OF INSPIRATION
"The Spirit of the Lord is upon me."

LECTURE VIII

THE MINISTRY OF INSPIRATION

WE have reached our final hour together, with a feeling on my part of not having said what I eagerly longed to say; with a wish that I could try it over again or had tried to say something else; with the temptation to attempt in this last hour to make up for what was lacking in the others. You will have this experience all through your ministry, as you near the proper end of your sermons. If you yield to the feeling you will plunge and struggle in a final effort of storm and stress, and you will ruin many a good conclusion by stretching it out to an unholy length. Let us pray now and always to be delivered from this depressing sensation and unreasonable endeavor.

I am wholly aware of the splendid topics which have been omitted from this list. You are aware of them yourselves. You can see that one of these omitted topics is the Ministry of Righteousness, another the Ministry of Power, and another the Teaching Ministry, to mention no more. Why were they not included? Because eight is eight and not ten. There is no other reason, except that a man is never wholly master of his own topics. Like a novelist's characters, they sometimes control him instead of obeying him.

In the topic for to-day we swing round to the heights again, with that other Minister. We started there with him. We close there with him. At the beginning the heavens opened and he came into view. At the end the heavens are still open so that we can see him. We are always thinking of him. Late in Mr. Lowell's life a friend found him studying Dante, and said: "Ah, Mr. Lowell, you are still studying Dante, I see." "Yes," said the poet, "always Dante, always Dante." With us it is always the Master, always the Master.

Let us recall again the fundamental basis of all we have said. If we had but one text, it would be this: "The kingdom of heaven is like." The kingdom of this heaven of our ministry is like the radiant kingdom of his. The supreme events in his history are both events that occurred and principles that abide, facts that were and principles to live by. They are not only significant in themselves, but also in what they have it in them to become, which is the real essence of evolution and development.

"What's excellent as God lives is permanent," not only as an indestructible fact, but as a living force. It was seen to be so with the vital themes that have already walked before us in his Person and ministry. It is not easy to live up to highest truths or to go the length of largest principles. We dread fanaticism, not seeing that the deadliest of all fanaticisms is the fanaticism of prudence, prudence that is afraid, the common sense that shrinks and fails to go up the heights where God can be seen face to face. But our lives and ministries can only be saved from feebleness and "a thousand peering littlenesses" by the power of an eternal life, by fresh, constant contact with the everlasting springs of great deeds, great truths, great principles, great persons, even the deeds, the truths, the principles, and the Person of the Highest himself. Let us not flinch, or turn back now in the application of our fundamental basis. This basis in its depth and reach underlies inspiration as it does incarnation and reconciliation. Inspiration also is an event and a principle, a thing that happened more than once and a principle that lives forevermore. It was an event for the men who spoke as they were moved by the Holy Ghost. They received their message at their highest from God, and gave it in the spirit for God. It was an event at Pentecost when the ancient prophecy was fulfilled in a new experience and promise for

speaking men and the life of man. It was an
event in the life of Isaiah when his lips were
touched for speaking, so that he spoke with
warmth, with illumination and with power. It
was an event in the life of Saint John when he
wrote, "We write these things in order that
our joy may be complete." Why multiply
words or instances? Inspiration as an event
we are ready to admit, to declare, to put into
our creeds, to defend as part of our deepest
faith. But inspiration as a principle also, a
principle that lives to be lived by, a principle
that preserves the continuity of Christian experience and binds the centuries together, inspiration to be expected and longed for by
modern men in religious work and speech, inspiration that makes the old inspiration intel-
ligible, this is not so clear an article of either
faith or experience. We believe in and are
familiar with unction and with earnestness, with
magnetism, with "muscular Christianity" and
the power to move, but we are not so well acquainted with anything that looks like inspiration. And the introduction of this subject
seems to our good sense to open a fair way to
mysticism, fanaticism, and even heresy. We
easily see the threatening shadows of religious
extravagance, and hear the names of well-
known groups of spiritual specialists. Very

well; I am not going to be diverted from an effort to find a right road because there are wrong ones. There is a truth here which is worth hunting for, a coin that has a lot of counterfeits because the real coin is so valuable. And this truth needs to be found. The age is not dying of too much real inspiration or spiritual life. The church is not too strong in a genuine strength begotten of the Holy Spirit. It has lots of might of other kinds, lots of power of other sorts, upon which it tends to rely. "Every church," says Hutton, "just now is living too much by its wits. Never did men in office in the church work harder. Never were church buildings so constantly in use. Never were appeals more insistent. Yet, at the best, 'having done all, we stand.' Such success as the churches may claim is not of the highest possible quality; it is too much fretted with anxiety and labor. It wants certain notes of peace, of fullness, of that confidence in God which has the victory over the world. It has a basis of worry and strain. It has enough to do with itself." Mr. Gladstone's sober words are not cheerful reading: "I am rather painfully impressed with the apprehension that the seen world is gaining upon the unseen. The vast expansion of its apparatus seems to have nothing to balance it. The church, which was the appointed instrument of the world's recovery, seems, taking all its branches together, rather unequal to its work."

The ministry is not too inspiring or too spiritual; its work is not overmuch in demonstration of the Spirit and of power. No matter whether it is more or less so than ever before, it is not enough so at this hour. It has eloquence, scholarship, and ability, magnetism and perfect elocution; it is filled with intense desire to do good; its men wear themselves out trying to lift and move people whose hearts have waxed gross; it is strong and faithful in the denunciation of evil personal and social. But there are too many sermons that have not a thrill in them, the ministry does not sufficiently speak with a power not its own, it has not the light of the Eternal on its face, it is not caught up into any heaven while it speaks, it does not set the breezes of another world blowing over men's spirits. The real way is worth finding if our ministry is to do its part in "keeping the soul of the world alive."

What, then, do we mean by a ministry of inspiration? How can it be obtained or created? How can it be preserved? And what will it do in the world? Free from all fanaticism and extravagance we sincerely desire this kind of ministry. In answering these questions let us not expect or attempt exact definitions. They are

278

the peril and the pitfall of much religious discussion. Here, as in other high matters, we shall get our best definitions, not in terms of the dictionary, but in terms of personal life. The person will define the term, and in a person the term will define itself. We shall best understand the thing by seeing it in personal action.

What, then, do we mean by a ministry of inspiration? Here, as everywhere, our conceptions and definitions should emerge at the highest levels, in the life of the best we know. What, then, did it mean in the case of that other Minister? With every allowance for what was unique and individual in him, we are more concerned to find what may be common to his life and ours. We ought not to be related to him solely or chiefly in the fact that he was tempted in all points as we are. That is not the best level. He was an inspiring person, in ways that do not seem magical, magnetic, or unnatural. This life of his in the heart of it looks like the proper, best way to build a personality. If we can find the secret of his life, we shall be well into the secret of our own. Inspiration in him does not seem to be just a divine afflatus, a lofty emotion, or the gift of infallibility. We have thought of it rather too much as the power that brings infallibility rather than the gift that brings life and vitality, spiritual insight, sensitiveness to truth and beauty, elevation of mind and heart, and responsiveness to God's spirit. It goes far deeper than any one thing or any partial experience. How, then, was it obtained by him? He surely was an inspiring personality, as every personality must be by reason of his constant, perfect, unbroken contact with God. There is no element of magic in it. It does not come upon men regardless, but upon the men who meet the conditions and pay the price. It is not lawless and capricious in its working, or in its coming, nor an arbitrary gift bestowed upon a chosen few. He never lost it. Such statements as "The words that I speak unto you, they are spirit, and they are life," "The Father that dwelleth in me, he doeth the works," carry us far. This is not simply an occasional outpouring upon his life, or spirit breathed into it once in a while; this shows a divine relation and a steady divine presence. We do not think it extravagant to say that he lived his life with God and in God, as he received it from God. We do not think it extravagant when Saint Paul says: "The life which I now live in the flesh I live by the faith of the Son of God." Why are we so afraid to go the length of our best truths? Arthur Brooks, speaking of his brother, Phillips Brooks, said: "God be praised to-day! From God he came;

with God he walked; God's world he loved;
God's children he helped; God's church he led;
God's blessed Son he followed; God's nearness
he enjoyed; with God he dwells." This branch
lived and bloomed and bore fruit, as all branches
must and will, by reason of the perfect union
with the sufficient source of life. No life can be
spiritual, can be inspired or inspiring, that does
not dwell in God, that does not have him
dwelling in it. The leaven must be in the meal,
the meal must be transformed by the leaven.
What one personality can do with another we
have not begun to measure. We have been in
bondage to materialistic, mechanistic or pietistic
standards and processes. What God can do in
nature and with nature we are only beginning to
see, to see as we get rid of certain false views
of his relation to nature and the character
of natural forces. But what the divine life
can do in the realm of human personality,
this we have seen once, and the vision makes
us long to see it again. We have seen once
what happens when a personality perfectly
gives itself up to be invested and invaded
by God, when his personality finds another
that makes perfect response to it. It is
vastly more than the contagion of goodness
or the thrill of a noble example. This is creative energy that makes such new creatures that

that other Minister can say to them, "Nothing shall be impossible to you"; that makes one of them say soberly, "It is God that worketh in us." For him as for all the supreme souls in our ministerial ancestry, inspiration is an experience, a fellowship, an everlasting communion which for him and all others makes their ministry sufficient.

The wealth, the character, and the use of his truth made another vital element in his inspiration. His lips were touched with a live coal, but they were lips worth touching. They could stand live coals. He was baptized with fire, but the fire fell upon abundant fuel. Many men pray for fire, divine fire, to descend upon them when they have no fuel that would give divine fire a chance to warm the world even if it did fall upon them. Many men gather fuel all their lives, great stacks of it, libraries full, heads full, manuscripts full, and never let any divine fire get anywhere near it. They keep it properly piled in regular order, sheltered and protected, exhibited and seasoned; or they just let it pile up in any kind of order or disorder, but no conflagration ever gets into it. It remains wood, wood to the end of time, never becoming warmth, never blazing with the divine flame, never leaving a deposit of ashes to show where once fire and fuel got together. Or men gather just one kind of fuel, and that never makes the best kind of a fire. We used to mix the beech, hard maple, oak, and hickory when we wanted a fire at its best. But the whole purpose of getting fuel together is not to have great piles of fuel, but that the chill shall be taken off the atmosphere of the world and the food of the world be cooked. Fire and fuel must get together. When shall we take a true view of our truth? When shall we think of it as Jesus thought of his? When shall we prize it for what it will do? For this is what makes truth valuable, not that it is abundant or admirable, but that it is useful in setting men free. Not the academic regard for truth, but the evangelistic use of it is our ideal. This made Jesus inspiring. He had the truths, all the truths, that released life, set forces free, and transformed character. The ministry always bears a feeble witness when its grasp upon truth is feeble or narrow or partial, or when it only has hold of one kind. Its witness is always feeble when its chief concern is for its truth, to possess it, to save it or to display it. Such preaching is always sounding brass and tinkling cymbals, preaching without any reach into life or any overwhelming hold upon life. A ministry with a feeble or narrow or partial truth can dazzle, can even blind men and deceive them as when one builds a bonfire of tissue paper, excelsior, shavings, hay, or stubble. But the ministry that inspires is the ministry that takes the supreme truths of life, of God's life and man's life, and plants them as living forces in the minds, the emotions, and the wills of men; the truths that open the heavens above men's heads and steady the earth beneath their feet. Little preaching of thin truth, noisy preaching of shallow truth, conceited preaching of showy truth will not do this. Men are inspired more by the walking of a living truth before them than by any sensuous appeal to emotion. Moved they may be by the thing that is moving; moved they may be by a contagion of enthusiasm, or by magnetism, by elocution, but they are inspired when supreme truth lays hold of their minds, stirs their souls and carries their wills into action. Lots of preaching makes men think, lots of it makes men feel, some of it makes men act, but the preaching that inspires does all of this in logical, living order.

Take the story of what happened at Pentecost. We may as well look at it here as later. The Spirit was upon that preacher, that fisherman of the common clay. He had the contact with the divine source of sufficiency and power. In the Spirit he told the whole splendid story of Jesus. That story was his truth. If you think telling it is intellectually easy, try it. If you want to stretch what brains you have, try preaching Christ. That is the supreme intellectual achievement. You have the whole story here: the Spirit of God in one preaching man, the rich, full truth spoken by that man, then the Spirit of God falling upon the listening men until they understood one another, until they had a new sense of God, were moved by a flaming passion for the common good and became brothers with a common stock of goods. That story is not a lesson in doctrine or economics, but a thrilling chapter in the history of preaching. Sit down with it until you are saturated with it, and maybe that which was spoken by Joel will come to pass again, for Pentecost is also an event and a principle, a thing that happened and a thing that happens when God has his way with men. It is easy to get the shallow, surface view of it and to vapor it away as the unthinking bystanders tried to with their silly talk about it. But I say to you that the preaching of our day, like the preaching of Peter on that great and notable day, must be in the same spirit, must use this same supreme truth that is in Jesus Christ, so that world confusion will become world understanding, racial confusion become racial harmony among the dwellers on the face of the earth, and so that the godless selfishness that godlessly says, "This is my stuff," will quit saying that and begin to say, "These are my brothers, and the stuff is ours." This is the dream that old men dream, this the vision that young men see. And nothing will bring it to pass again but the kind of preaching that once brought it to pass. The men who do this supreme thing must have the spirit and the far-reaching truth that centers in Jesus. Pulpits without the spirit and without the living truth will be useless and helpless in the face of the modern world, which is the ancient world emphasized. The word that is void and lifeless in its utterance returns void to its source. Religious conditions, racial conditions, moral conditions, material conditions as they were that day at Pentecost are so suggestive of modern conditions that the story lays hold of thoughtful men like a prophecy. In all its features Pentecost looks like an event and a principle, like a thing that occurred and a principle that lives. It called then, it calls now, for a ministry adequate through inspiration with sufficient spirit and with potent truth.

His possession of truth and his use of truth both make him a minister of inspiration. There ought to be an extra classification of men based upon the way they use the truth they have. Instantly you will think of the men who use

their truth in vulgar display, of the men who
use it for their own advantage or profit, of the
men who use it for purposes of rebuke and denunciation, of the men who use truth as the
basis of argument and controversy, to name no
others. Or you think of the artist's use, the
philosopher's use, the scientist's use, the mer-
chant's use of truth. Not all of it is improper,
of course, but not any of it is on the same level
with Jesus's use of truth, not any of it inspires
as his use does. With the purpose of redemption ruling his life he used truth ever for life's
sake, ever to set life free and to make life holy.
No truth was too precious for such use; indeed, it
was precious only because of such use. No life
was too lowly to be lifted by the truth that
came out of the skies. What he said to Nicodemus, to the woman at the well, or to poor
Zacchæus was not simply the statement of a
doctrine. It was the sure bringing of supremest
truth to neediest life for life's sake. It was a
thrilling lesson in the ministry of redemption.
An English journalist says of an English archbishop: "He is an embodied office. You never
catch him without the lawn sleeves. You never
surprise him out of the clerical and courtly accent." Well, that other Minister is an embodied Redeemer. You never catch him without the cross and the word of redemption. You

never surprise him out of the redeeming accent.
We are so careless, so reckless, in our use of our
highest truths. We do not speak falsely, of
course, but we are too easily caught out of
character. The ministry must bear the double
test of inspiration—the possession of truth and
the use of truth—even as his ministry did.

His ministry was a ministry of inspiration, as
ours must be by reason of the consecration of
his life to the things he had to do. This constitutes "the breed of noble blood"; not clever-
ness, nor energy, nor talent, but this divine,
unhesitating, unresting consecration. This alone
lights the lamps that burn with strong and
steady flame. This is religious genius, respond-
ing to the murmurs and agonies of men. "Knowing whence he came," fully conscious of his ancestry; "knowing whither he went," fully aware
of his destiny, he girded himself and washed the
feet of the weary and travel-worn. Heredity is
an inspiring thing, not when it is asserted, but
when in such ways it is consecrated. Destiny
is glorious, not when it is exhibited in vanity,
but when it is set to service. Long ago the
prophet drew the picture of a person like this:
"A man shall be as an hiding place from the
wind, and a covert from the tempest; as rivers
of water in a dry place, as the shadow of a great
rock in a weary land." Then in a single life,

full, true, complete manhood walked across the
wide world in such devotion and service that
the spoken word became a living word before
men's eyes. This also was an event and a
principle; an event in one life, a principle for
all life. He did not look for inspiring people to
work with, inspiring congregations to preach to.
He brought his life, his words, his deeds to the
dull, the hard, the sodden, and the uninspiring;
and when unbelief blocked his way he went
away heavy-hearted. When poor John the
Baptist got all mixed up on a question of the
evidences of Christianity, bothered almost to
death about a question of apologetics, Jesus
sent him word something like this: "I know
whence I came. I know whither I go. Inspiration and divine origins are not matters of argument, but of experience and demonstration. The
blind are receiving their sight, John; the lame
are walking, lepers are being cleansed, the deaf
are hearing the voices of their friends, the dead
are being raised up, and the poor, the outcasts,
have good news preached to them. Doubt no
more."

He does not prove his deity by asserting it,
even in such words as "I and my Father are
one," but by keeping perfect step with God in
the service of mankind, by daily showing that
he can do and will do the things that God is

doing. And this both proves and reveals his deity.

And that other Minister made an atmosphere of consecration just as some men make an atmosphere of belief, others an atmosphere of doubt, others an atmosphere of benevolence, and others still an atmosphere of skepticism and selfishness. It was said of General Kleber that it made men brave just to look at him. It was said of another: "His very presence had power to carry happiness to hearts that were heavy. It was a dull, rainy day when things looked dark and lowering, but Phillips Brooks came down Newspaper Row and all was bright." It was said of a recent American novelist that the young men and women of his time lived with happier bravery because of him. Maclaren says that when Henry Drummond entered a room his presence seemed to change the temperature. Jesus created an atmosphere of rapturous consecration. "I must be about my Father's business." "My meat is to do the will of him that sent me." "I do always those things that please him." These are not the sentences of a man boasting. These are the words of a man describing his life and its principles. He does not talk of consecration much. He holds no special meetings for it. It is not occasional or special with him. It is the basis of his entire life. And I see no way to take any other view of life except to take a lower view. You can do that if you will. You can cut the heart out of his influence upon you by dropping to a lower plane. But you take all the meaning out of such words as these when you do not live clear up to them. "I am come that they might have life." "He that believeth on the Son hath everlasting life." One man gives himself to another. The power and courage, the faith and hope of one pass into another. That is the way he gives us life. That makes his life inspiring again, as when God breathed into man and he ceased to be a dull, lifeless thing and became a living soul. And like that in its essence a consecrated life always works. You cannot give what you have not got. You cannot create consecration unless you have consecration. You cannot cause men to do their best unless you live at your best. Learning will not do it. Eloquence will not do it. Even brilliant deeds will not do it. Life giving is in the hands of life possessors. We have seen such men. We know such men, in large groups and small ones. They bring vitality, they create it. They bring consecration, they create it. They bring the inspiration of perfect devotion, glad and rapturous. They create it because they have it.

GOOD MINISTERS OF JESUS CHRIST

The ministry of that other Minister was inspiring because of his personality. This was his supreme gift to men. It is the supreme achievement. You may think this is dangerous ground. It is, but it is chiefly dangerous ground to keep away from. I do not forget how Horace Bushnell, for apologetic purposes, declared that "the character of Jesus forbids his possible classification with men," but there is another apologetic also in the words "the imitableness of Christ's character." We exalt him not by setting him apart, even though we set him on high. We crown him when we set him within, when we have him formed in us, when we put him on as a garment. Of course, we cannot expect to possess sinlessness like his, but by grace we may expect and achieve sanctity even like his, for what he achieved was as regal as what he possessed by inheritance. And we are always more concerned with our resemblances to him than with our differences from him. We make constant allowance for what was unique in him, but even as we do it we draw as close as we can that we may be renewed in the same image. What was good in him cannot be bad in us.

Now, character and personality are not vague terms. Character is something more than characteristics, personality something more than qualities. But character is made up of characteristics and personality is made up of qualities. Many writers have analyzed that other Minister. Here is one list, which could be matched by others: "The characteristics of Jesus are strength, sincerity, reasonableness, poise, originality, narrowness, breadth, trust, brotherliness, optimism, chivalry, firmness, generosity, candor, enthusiasm, gladness, humility, patience, courage, indignation, reverence, holiness, and greatness." And personality, says another, is made up of four qualities, "consciousness of self, consciousness of power, consciousness of obligation, consciousness of determination." It says, "I am, I can, I ought, I will." The list is pretty long, but might easily be longer. And each of these qualities is good when combined with all the others. The absence of any one of them would not make a better character. Nor would it help any to let any one of these characteristics get top-heavy. Character and civilization both go wrong when one element dominates all the rest. And if these qualities were all good in him, would they not be equally good in us? No wonder he was an inspiring personality, being this kind. No wonder so many of us are so uninspiring, not being this kind in any large measure. Most of us have some of these characteristics, but lack the others. Some of us

have faith, but not much goodness; some have
goodness, and not much knowledge; some have
knowledge, accurate and encyclopedic, but not
much self-control. Some have self-control, but
not much brotherly affection; and some have
brotherly affection—they are good fellows—but
not much love. So on you can go. Jesus is the
living definition of the kind of manhood that inspires manhood, character that inspires and
creates character, a ministry of inspiration not
because of some magical or magnetic quality,
but because of that kind of character which by
God's grace and power enables us to say, "Now
are we the sons of God." The roots of his life
ran back to God, the fruit of his life came from
God, the flower of it came out in consecration and
character. Have I made my meaning clear? Do
we see what made his life inspiring, so that we
also see what makes any life inspiring? Its
contact with God; its source and deepest root
in God; its vital possession and redemptive use
of truth, the truth as it was in Jesus Christ,
the truth that sets men free; its eternal consecration to the will of God and the weal of the
world, and, finally, its likeness to God in all
those qualities that make in any world or any
age, that make in any person, divine or human,
a perfect character and an inspiring personality.
I am not thinking much of the life to come, but

am appealing to you to "pitch this one high."
I have not argued for the deity of Jesus, though
it is the center and strength of my life and faith,
but am crying out to you,

> "Ah, let us try
> If we then too can be such men as he."

For this is our assurance: "In him we live, and
move, and have our being," and

> "God's greatness flows round our incompleteness,
> Round our restlessness, his rest."

How does one keep on being inspiring? The
preservation of a noble quality is quite as important as the getting of it. Even our best
possessions deteriorate, our highest experiences
become stale, unless they are used aright. Holiness itself becomes rancid when it is treated
exclusively as a personal experience or emotion.
It saves itself by becoming righteousness which
is holiness in action, holiness at work, holiness
healing lepers, opening blind eyes and washing
disciples' feet. The branches that do not bear
have to be cut off at last, bearing being the condition of retaining the connection with the
source of life. One keeps on being inspired and
inspiring by making the outflow of spiritual life
and power equal at least to the intake, by keeping the means and the ends of experience in
proper balance, by the use he makes of the

qualities that inspire him. Services must always equal visions if visions are to continue to any man. This thing cannot be had once for all and kept indefinitely, no matter where it is put or how it is kept. It will not keep if kept sealed, in a cool place. It must always be kept open, in places warm with human life. We have no tragedies sadder or more tragic than the tragedies of lost inspirations, real "lights that failed." They were genuine and large once in the lives of certain men in our ministry. Then those ministries became commercialized, or spoiled by prosperity, or soured by adversity, or stifled with worldliness, or honeycombed by personal evil, or weakened by age, and the inspiration ceased. The men went on using the words they once had used, but no longer with power over life. For you can speak with the tongues of men and angels and still make nothing but a noise in the world.

Nor is this a thing you can have for occasional use. Some sermons will be better than others, some occasions more notable than others, but the qualities that make you a minister of inspiration cannot be put on and off at will, used lavishly before great congregations and withheld from small ones, poured out upon inspiring gatherings and reserved from the assemblies that are wholly uninspiring. A minister keeps his inspiration by the words he speaks, by the deeds he performs, by the spirit he lives in and lives out, by the way he meets all life's experiences, the so-called common and the so-called extraordinary, the raging, overwhelming crises of temptation and the small, ugly, subtle, nibbling at his moral life which goes on unsuspected by all save himself. Peter's inspiration was clear at Pentecost, and slipped in the presence of a simple maid in the hour of his Master's trial. The slipping is not a lovely spectacle in his life or any other.

Open and reread again the story of one or two incidents in that other Minister's life. Take the scene of his baptism. Down into the historic river he went to fulfill every religious duty and to observe the proper religious sacraments. Others had done it, he would do it, to set his life in closest relation with theirs by every possible act. And he was baptized of water. And the heavens opened, and the Spirit descended and the voice said: "This is my Son, dearly loved, in whom I delight." At the transfiguration the heavens opened again and the voice said, "Thou art my son, in whom I am well pleased." By riverside and on mountain top, to him and to others of him, those words were spoken. And I cannot doubt that in many other hours they were repeated to him, in hours when he needed this assurance. For he did not lose the testimony that he pleased God. Do you see, need I go on? *"He* will baptize *you* not many days hence," and you will hear in your inmost soul those words spoken to him when the heavens opened. For you cannot go on into this ministry or in this ministry with inspiration unless the Spirit comes upon you also, unless you also know that you are well-loved sons of God. How can you make known to other men, to men in every land, their sonship in Jesus Christ unless you have entered into his experience with him and know yourselves to have true sonship? How are you going to fight wild beasts at Ephesus, cast out demons, climb shining heights to see God face to face unless you also shall be reassured again and again that you are God's sons and that he cares for you? This also is an event and a principle in the far, deep, personal reaches of it.

Baptized, not to ecstasy, not to religious rapture, but to his public ministry and personal life, he goes almost at once into the wilderness to have it out with the tempter of his life and ours. Carlyle put it thus: "To me nothing seems more natural than that the Son of man . . . . should be carried of the Spirit into grim solitudes, and there fronting the tempter do grimmest battle with him. . . . Name it as we choose, with or without visible devil, whether in the wilderness or populous moral desert of selfishness and baseness—to such temptation as we are all called." If you read this story with your hearts, you will be shouting before you are through. It is peculiarly and preeminently a picture of personal experience for us minister men. Hardly anything in Jesus's whole life is more truly both event and principle than his experience there in the wilderness, where he fought out for himself and for us at least three fundamental issues. These are not temptations to vulgar, low-down evil. These are the tests that supreme souls, the best souls must meet between the consecration of their lives and the living of their lives; between their ordination under the open heavens and their ministry in an open world. Not to lust, to murder, to drunkenness or to theft are these solicitations, but to those spiritual experiences that test the heart of a ministry in Jesus's time or ours. How will you, who have been baptized with God's power, use that power? Will you use it on your advantage or save it for your task? Will you make bread for yourself, or will you make bread for others? Will you save yourselves or save others? You cannot do both. He could not do both. Which do you mean to do? Will you put the test of success upon a material or upon a spiritual

basis? How shall we tell men to live, upon
bread alone, or upon every word from God?
How shall we live ourselves? What did that
other Minister answer to all these questions?
No wonder the voice from heaven said, "This
is my Son." No wonder either that it added,
"Hear him." A minister like that, using his
power in that fashion, deserves to be heard.

How shall we use God's promises? How shall
we get a hearing? Shall we throw ourselves
down before the crowds to test God's promises,
to see whether they are true? Shall we make a
display, a merchandise of our sonship? Shall we
call upon the angels to save us while we engage
in these vulgar theatrics? Or shall we trust
God and his promises without putting him to
these tests? Shall we get our hearing, not by
the display of our piety, but by the worth of
our message? And shall we only call upon the
angels to help us while we are walking in the
path of obedience and duty? Jesus seemed so
very sure of God, so sure of him that he would
not put him to a test. And he had his reward.
Angels do not care much for men treating God
with question and test. But it is the business
of the universe to have angels at hand to keep
such a minister as Jesus from dashing his foot
against a stone while he walks in the way of
faith and service.

THE MINISTRY OF INSPIRATION

How will you try to win your world, near and far, the world spread out to large view and the world of the narrow limits? Will you try to win it by going over to it, by compromise with it, conformity to it, by bowing down to it? Maybe you can dodge the cross that way. Maybe you can follow Him without denying yourself or taking up your cross daily. Maybe you can get a wide reputation for shrewdness, worldly wisdom, and hard-headed common sense, as of a man who has his feet on the ground, and is not a visionary. You will not be called a fanatic, nor your life-story be told under the title, "A Singular Life," if you try this. You will escape the crucifixion that comes for righteousness sake if you do it this way. Or when you come face to face with the question, will you tell all the devils of compromise with evil, of bargain with wrong, of worship of success no matter how won, that you will have none of them, that they are to get behind you and stay out of sight, that you have resisted selfishness and presumption and will not yield to compromise? You cannot win your world and worship it. He could not. You cannot. Which things are an event and a principle, an event that makes a minister's heart hammer with courage and hope, an event that creates faith and courage and resolution to keep life from evil; a principle that throws itself into the centuries with the power of a life blameless and endless. Nothing that He did was more inspired or more inspiring than this. For a man needs to be inspired to meet such crucial crises in his life. And a man who meets them in this manner is inspiring to all other men who take him seriously. If the angels had any interest in Jesus, they must have watched the steps of this experience with breathless interest and rapturous delight. They must have sung when he refused to call upon them to save him from unwarranted test, but they must have come on swiftest wing to minister to him when the battle was won. The devil will tempt you as the devil tempted him. But you can determine whether, when it is over, the devil will remain in possession of the field of your soul, or whether the devil will leave and the angels will come. And the world of tempted men, men battling for their souls, battling in the realm of high principles, battling in the heart of life, battling at its depths and on its heights will have courage or fear, bravery or cowardice, will win or lose, not on the basis of what you say about temptation, but on the basis of the way you meet it. Nothing that Jesus could have said would have had a particle of creative power in it, an iota of inspiration to other men, if he had talked wisely and broken weakly at any of these points.

And the devil left him and the angels came, and I doubt not they said over and over to him, "Thou art God's Son, men will hear you." And men do. For we can tell his story in the colleges and let this record loose in the world of men. This is the royal way minister men ought to meet temptation. This is the way they ought to use their power, use God's promises, get their hearing and win their world. Nobody wants you to sell out, either to your own selfishness, or to your fear, or to the devil himself. And when you strike step with that other One there, when men see the two of you walking that way of victory together, walking that way which makes sure that other men will be fed, no matter about you; that God's promises will be used in the path of duty, that the devil is beaten again at his own game, then men will know that the real ministry has come again to the world. And you need not be surprised to have one and another gratefully say to you, "Dominie, we know that you are a preacher come from God, for no one lives this kind of life except God be with him."

I cannot go on, alluring as this is to me. I dare not think that I have made clear what I wanted to make clear in this study of the ministry of inspiration. This awful feeling of failure will burden your souls as you come to the end of sermons on such themes as this. Shall we remember to-day, and always, for our comfort, the reality, the nearness, the inward presence of that Holy Spirit which forever helps our infirmities, so that listening men will catch the vision of a spiritual life, and long to live it, even though you have stumbled through the discussion of it. So I dare hope it may be to-day. Our sufficiency is not of rhetoric or logic, after all, but of God.

And far more than we, he desires to have a ministry of inspiration in the earth in this our day. He sees how the world has come in its new Exodus toward the land of promise to the bitter waters of Marah again, the waters that do not taste good to the soul of man. He longs, as aforetime, that his ministers shall throw the living branch of healing into these bitter waters of the world, that men shall drink in the desert, go forward in the march, and not die. He sees the world always going one of two ways, from worldliness into more worldliness, or from worldliness into some more spiritual, ethical way of life for men and the world. He knows that always it has been the men of inspiration who have set the currents the right way. He knows what has been done in all the centuries by lofty souls, not a few, by his Son above all, to make him real to men, to make their own souls real to them, and he waits to make a new ministry of power and inspiration to make him real again. He knows how prophets and evangelists, men known to the world, men unknown to wide circles, have by the Spirit lifted other men above narrowness, above complacency, above low ideals and low outlooks, above their sins even, and have created hope and courage, given comfort and strength, and have been as the shadow of a great rock in a weary land. He is eager to see again the working of the miracle that inspiring personalities have always worked upon other personalities. For this is the miracle that he cares to see repeated in the world, the miracle of life renewing and transforming life. He had one Son in whom he was always pleased. His heart yearns over us that we shall be such sons as shall please him again. Shall we disappoint him?

Once a simple woman said to a prophet, "I know that thou art a man of God." Once again people took knowledge of some others that they had been with Jesus and learned of him. Our Father seeks again men of whom that can be said with truth.

So, to make us ministers of inspiration, he gives us his Spirit, gives us his truth, consecrates our lives and perfects our personalities. So, to keep us inspiring, he keeps us at work, ties us up with all human need, makes us his sons, fights our battles with us and for us, keeps us from evil and makes us men like that other Minister in whom he was always well pleased. This is our joy as we older men think sadly of such poor ministry as we have had. This is our joy as we think hopefully of such glorious ministry as you may have in the world. The war will not always last. It will not always be the center of conversation, the disturbing fact in all thought. The world must be rebuilt in righteousness and peace, in truth and brotherhood, in love and holiness. There is no other name under heaven whereby it can be restored than the name that is above every name. There is no other service beyond the service a Christlike ministry can render, must render, to Christ's world. The day of the ministry is disturbed and difficult, but not gone. Many heads are weary, many hearts faint, but the power of an endless life is in your Master and from him in you. Rise, let us be going, to be inspiring voices "in the rich dawn of an ampler day," not to be ministered unto, but to minister and to give our lives for the ransom of men, to touch souls beset with fear, crushed with woe, bereft of love, despoiled by evil, with the power of the creative Christ, so that faith and hope and love may be born again in the lives of men. And they will say as of old it was said, an "angel came again, and waked me, as a man that is wakened out of his sleep." Thus shall the good ministry of Jesus Christ bring to pass the fulfillment of the ancient words: "Hereafter ye shall see the heavens open, and the angels of God ascending and descending." Much of our ministry lies behind us; most of yours lies before you. See that ye abound in all these graces that are his and yours.

I Standard :- P. 18-19. Ministry of Jesus.

II Aim :- Our concern is emphatically with the minister who is preacher to a congregation and pastor to a community.

A. Revelation :- God's nearness - His way with Authority :- Bible record of revelation. Know God :- be like him :- show him as he is.

B. Redemption :-